PREYING ON THE ELDERLY

THE ART OF SCAMMING THE ELDERLY IN JAPAN

DAISUKE SUZUKI

TRANSLATED BY BERNARD SUSSER

 CDG Books

Melbourne – London – Tokyo – New York

CDG Books

www.cdg-books.com

447 Broadway, 2nd Floor #393, New York NY, 10013, United States
4th Floor, Silverstream House, 45 Fitzroy Street Fitzrovia, London W1T 6EB,
   United Kingdom
Ground Level, 470 St Kilda Road, Melbourne, Victoria 3004, Australia
2nd Floor, Daiya Building, 2-2-15 Hamamatsu-cho, Minato-ku, Tokyo
   105-0013, Japan

ROJIN GUI – KOREISHA WO NERAU SAGI NO SHOTAI
Copyright © SUZUKI Daisuke 2015
Original Japanese edition published by Chikumashobo Ltd., Tokyo
This English edition arranged with Chikumashobo Ltd.

Information on this title:
www.castledown.com/cdg-books/view-title/?reference=9781954623071

DOI: 10.29140/9781954623071

Preying on the Elderly: The Art of Scamming the Elderly in Japan

English translation © SUZUKI Daisuke, 2023
Translated by Bernard Susser

Typeset by Castledown Design, Melbourne
ISBN: 978-1-954623-07-1 (Paperback)
ISBN: 978-1-954623-08-8 (Digital)

Contents

Introduction

According to the National Police Agency's 2013 White Paper,[1] approximately 80% of the victims of special fraud[2] crimes, including remittance scams, were elderly. Every year the record for the worst year for total losses is broken; in the first 11 months of 2014, losses reached 49,873.43 million yen. Further, concerning crimes related to specified commercial transactions,[3] so-called fraudulent business practices such as solicitation for moneymaking schemes involving contracts for unlisted shares and public corporation bonds, etc., door-to-door sales, unscrupulous house renovation contractors, and sales methods using hypnosis, more than 70% of the consultations at consumer centers nationwide about these as well are from the elderly. Specifically, 71.5% of consultations concerning crimes related to solicitation for moneymaking schemes, and 77.9 % of consultations relating to specified commercial transactions crimes, are from the elderly.

At present, crimes of fraud and fraudulent business practices preying on the elderly are increasing by leaps and bounds. In fact, preying on the elderly is in an age of a hundred flowers blooming. But why is this the case? There are so many people who make their living deceiving the elderly, who originally had been deserving of respect. Have the Japanese people lost their virtue? Have they no sense of what is wrong? After all, everyone has parents and grandparents. Are they so heartless? It's frightening.

I want to ask the elderly themselves who say that they are not responsible, "Have you ever considered that the

[1] More recent data can be found in National Police Agency. (2020). *The White Paper on Police 2020 (Digest Edition)*, pp. 2-3. https://www.npa.go.jp/hakusyo/r02/english/Section1.pdf

[2] Special fraud crimes: *tokushū sagi* (also called "specialized frauds") include remittance, billing, advance-fee loan, and refund frauds.

[3] Specified commercial transactions: *tokuteishō torihiki.*

cause of those criminals targeting you elderly people lies with you yourselves?"

It is easy to imagine the reaction to this question. Today's elderly are the ones who rebuilt Japan splendidly from the postwar ruins. Grudging sleep, they worked tirelessly, raising children, building roads and buildings, and developing industries; they raised Japan from a defeated nation into a world-famous economic superpower. They would say that we rebuilt this country and finally retired to pass the remainder of our days; why should the reason lie with us that the wealth we have accumulated through a lifetime of hard work is being targeted?

Very true. Quite right. However, no matter how much that correct argument is brandished, however much the police try to eradicate such crimes, preying on the elderly will continue. This is my frank impression after investigating the perpetrators of these crimes.

My main topic as an investigative journalist has been young people who have been raised in underprivileged family environments, subject to poverty, abuse, or abandonment, and who have come to live on the underside of society. My work as a journalist has been to draw out the feelings of young offenders and perpetrators of crimes, placing primary importance on revealing the pain and suffering felt by those who have been detested by society. What I learned was that with no appropriate education, parental love, or protection from society in their youth, they were drawn into criminal organizations. However, concerning those who prey on the elderly, I cannot say that they are necessarily criminals bred by such poverty in birth and upbringing. Some have received sufficient parental love. Some are university educated. Even so, they clearly harbor hostile feelings toward the elderly and bare their fangs at them. Why?

Having interviewed young people who have dirtied their hands in special fraud crimes, of which preying on the elderly may be the most typical, I feel that they are the "night dew" generation. Encountering them brings to mind a desert at night. Try to imagine this. These young people are thirsty in a desert. There is nothing around them but a parched oasis and a dried-up well. There is no sign of rain, and they have no strength left to dig a new well. They can only suck up the night dew to relieve their thirst. However, right next to them are people holding straw bags filled with water. These are the elderly.

These old people probably give water to their own children and grandchildren, but they never give water to other young people. They do not even lend out water. If the elderly spared these young people just a little water, they would probably be able to dig their own wells and make their own oases. But they do not, so what will happen? The young people, with bloodshot eyes and parched with thirst, sooner or later will grab the bags of water that the elderly are holding. Isn't it self-evident?

I want to dispel an important misunderstanding. It is not the case that crimes targeting the elderly take advantage of the fact that the elderly are vulnerable. These crimes are the blades of an insurrection by young people who are overwhelmingly inferior economically against the elderly who are overwhelmingly their economic superiors.

The well-off elderly might say that however thirsty young people are, Japan today is an advanced nation and there is no poverty that necessitates stealing or robbing because one has no food. However, I have been forced to conclude that that is a misreading of the times. The present is not like the period of high economic growth when endeavor was always rewarded. However hard they try, young people have no assurance of a stable future. The previous generation had the dream that even if they had only a crust of bread to eat today, they could eat a full-course meal if only they tried hard. The present generation is full of resignation that they are eating only a crust of bread today but even if they try hard, they will have to live on bread crusts their whole lives. In terms of the degree of thirst, today's young people are probably thirstier than the postwar poor.

There are no official statistics but in talking to contemporary college students I have been surprised. Many students tell me, "After I graduate, I will repay my parents the tuition and allowance they sent me while I was a student." I myself was born in 1973 as a member of the second postwar baby boom,[4] the grueling entrance exam hell generation, and the employment ice age[5] generation, but when I think of it now, I believe that I was really lucky. At least in my generation, the idea of "repaying allowances to parents" was not so common.

If we need concrete data, there is the issue of the postgraduation poverty of students who had student loans. The number of former student loan holders who were brought to court because they were unable to repay their student loans was 58 in 2004 but increased explosively more than 100 times to 6,193 in 2012. Their feelings of despair and sense of helplessness are without parallel.

Among them, young people with new appellations such as "mild *yankī* " and "soft *yankī* "[6] are drawing attention. Harada Yōhei, a marketing analyst at Hakuhōdō, has described them as a social class that values not a lifestyle seeking a high income and career advancement, but a lifestyle in which parents and siblings, and those around them of their own generation, all mutually support each other, even if their income is low. In other words, they are resigned to their fate.

The young people who prey on the elderly are the ones who have broken through this outrageously thick cloud of paralysis and helplessness. Some are from impoverished households, some were raised in impoverished local towns that appear to have been abandoned by our centralized, urbanized society, and some even went to university but

---

[4] The "second postwar baby boom" took place in the early 1970s.

[5] "'Employment ice age,' roughly 1993-2005, when many job seekers could not find the kind of jobs they wanted, eventually leaving the labor force and remaining marginalized." The Japan Institute for Labour Policy and Training. (2016). *Labor Situation in Japan and Its Analysis: General Overview 2015/2016*, p. 14. http://www.jil.go.jp/english/lsj/general/2015-2016/1-2.pdf

[6] *"Yankī"* (Yankee) means "juvenile delinquent"; Harada Yōhei argued that recently delinquents have become soft or mild. See *The Growing Ranks of Japan's "Mellow Rebels."* (2014). Nippon.com. http://www.nippon.com/en/in-depth/a03202/

are struggling to find a job.

What they have in common is that they are extremely talented and are almost pathologically motivated. They continue to resist, neither tamed nor crushed by feelings of despair. There are blood and tears. They are the type of people who embrace such human passions excessively.

Preying on the elderly already has become highly organized, and these young people are being trained to sharpen their fangs; systems are in place to support them in criminal acts, using their high motivation. In a sense, they are "economic guerrillas." With the same resentment in their breasts as that of the people of medieval times who brandished their blades at the aristocratic classes who were indifferent to their poverty and suffering, they take the lead in preying on the elderly.

This book is not a guide to preventing the crime of preying on the elderly. A reader who simply wants to know how the elderly can protect themselves need not buy this book. However, I believe that if you continue reading, you will come to understand that whatever preventative measures are taken, preying on the elderly will not cease as long as this "class society" exists. Even if special fraud crimes disappear, these young people will continue to bare their fangs at the elderly by other means.

Also, these are not crimes that strike at the weakness of the elderly's capacity to make decisions. They have developed perfectly logical arguments to deceive the elderly and take their money. Now, even those in the prime of life, with their full mental and physical capacities, cannot rest easy. They are marked as targets to be preyed on in the future.

This book records fully the actual image of young people living in this situation and their glowing passion.

Note:

To convey as accurately as possible the atmosphere of the sites that prey on the elderly, the people involved, and their extremely complicated organizational structure, I have frequently used fictional descriptions, but these are all based on themes from interviews with the actual persons concerned, so this book can be considered almost completely nonfiction. There is always an actual model for each person who appears in the book.

Translator's notes:

1) All footnotes have been added by the translator.
2) The speeches in quotation marks use slang and other speech forms associated with gangsters. I have not attempted to translate these into any patois associated with American gangsters.
3) Japanese names are given in the Japanese order: family name, then given name.
4) Japanese words that are ambiguous with regard to sex have been translated consistently into the masculine gender.
5) The translator would like to acknowledge the very useful suggestions and corrections made by Dr. Chika Fujimoto, editor at Castledown.

Chapter 1

Who preys on the elderly? The frightening methods of scams targeting the elderly

1.1 Young people who look like company employees

The area around T Station, less than 30 minutes by train from central Tokyo, appears to be going downhill. There is a drugstore, a coffee shop, a beef bowl shop, etc., along the rotary in front of the station, but the supermarket looks to be closed, with notices announcing "out of business" on its shutters. Prominent are two- or three-storied commercial buildings with big vacancy signs; the only place of amusement near the station is a non-chain-affiliated karaoke box with open hours an unenterprising 11:00 a.m. to 11:00 p.m.

However, in a complete change from that town's unprosperous appearance, a large parking lot is crammed with bicycles, showing that this place has become a bed-room community for people working in central Tokyo or the neighboring factory belt. Looking at the rental notices in the window of the real estate agent in front of the station, we can see that this area around T Station is blessed with very cheap rental properties in comparison to the wider area.

7:40 a.m. Many commuters, looking tired and dragging their feet, are making their way along the road to the station. However, there are some young men moving in the opposite direction as if pushing their way through this crowd. In their twenties to early thirties, wearing subdued suits with leather shoes to match, their black hair is cut short and combed. They have no fashionable piercings and wear no fashion accessories. They look like models for pictures of steady company employees but for some reason their gaze is piercing.

Do these rapidly walking young men work for the same

company? Perhaps, but for some reason, even if their eyes meet, they just give a slight nod and say nothing. The place that draws them in is an old, five-story office building with leased commercial space about a five-minute's walk from the station at the intersection of a national highway and the street that runs from the station.

Facing the highway, where the morning rush hour continues, this building, jammed between a family restaurant and a convenience store, is old but trim and well taken care of. Looking at the aluminum nameplates showing the tenants, we find a law office, a small trading company, an Internet sales company, and so on.

The office where these young men who look like company employees work is on the third floor. However, when one of them gets on the elevator, he does a strange thing. To push the button for the third floor, he balls his fist and pushes it with the second knuckle of his middle finger, knocking it with a thump. The next young man to enter the elevator does the same, thump.

Before 7:50 the young men who look like company employees have entered the office, punched their time-cards, and lined up in a single file in front of the white-board next to the windows. The office is plain; in addition to the whiteboard, there are just three sets of simple conference tables and chairs, separated from each other by partitions. When they are all lined up, a man who arrived before any of the others steps in front. This man, who seems to be in charge of this office, might be in his thirties. His name is Dokugawa. Dressed in a conservative business suit, his gaze seems to be more piercing than any of the others there. Taking a deep breath, Dokugawa begins the morning briefing.

"Good morning!!" As his loud voice reverberates around the room, the young men return his greeting in voices as loud as his: "Good morning!"

"Good. Today, let's begin with inspection of personal belongings. Everyone check the person next to him. We've done this many times, so you know the drill. The only things you're allowed to bring in here are cigarettes, your work phone, and cash. Remember, I'll beat the shit out of anybody who's got anything that shows your identity, like a license, credit card, or a cell phone in your own name." As his forceful voice, deep and threatening, hardly imaginable from his refined businessman's appearance, echoed around the room, the young men meticulously began to check each other's briefcases, suit pockets, and so on. But this took only a short time, not even a minute, because most of them had nothing but cash and a cell phone.

Having confirmed that nobody had broken the rules, Dokugawa again made an appeal in a loud voice. "All right, before we start work, let's do the usual cheer. Everyone, stand at attention!"

Just like an army, the young men stood up straight, clasped their hands together behind their backs, and began to chant following the leader, who chanted this slogan in a loud voice: "The nine prohibitions: Liquor! Drugs! Women! Gambling! Fighting! Sidelines! Attire! Family! Banks!"

You could see Dokugawa pointing to slips of colored paper held by magnets on the whiteboard, on which the items of this incantation had been written in large letters with a broad felt tip marker. As Dokugawa shouted out the items the young men repeated them after him, but nobody so much as looked at the colored papers, probably because they had already memorized them; instead, they looked straight ahead.

"OK, let's get to work!"

"Let's get to work!"

At Dokugawa's command, they finally began work. The young men, their expressions still tense, sat down at the conference tables and opened the folders in front of them. There were three teams of three men each.

"How far did we get yesterday?"

"I think that we were in the 80s."

Next to those talking in low voices were some who twisted their necks while saying "Ah, Ah, Ah" as if they were practicing vocalization. Dokugawa walked around the room, leaving one cell phone and plastic bottles of drinks at each of the three tables.

1.2 Who are they targeting?

Just what kind of company do you think this is?

In fact, this is the scene every morning at a cell (local office of a perpetrator group) for the "It's me" scam (swindling money by a phone call pretending to be a family member or relative); this is the most standard among the special fraud crimes that continue to cause increasing losses even now. This depiction is based on my interviews with a former *bantō* [CEO or president] of an "It's me"[7] scam group. The young men who look like businessmen are called "players" in this situation; they are the ones who call the victims. They are unseen at the other end of the phone line, committing crimes of fraud that continue to shake the world.

The first time I could investigate just how this kind of scam cell was managed was about 2009; I still cannot forget the culture shock I received then. It goes without saying that fraud is a crime and the people who are involved with such an organization are criminals; that office itself seems a different world where those young men hanging out there looked like gang members who could have just stepped out of a manga. This is just what anyone would think; I too felt the same the first time I met members of that fraud cell.

However, the more I listened to what the people actually working there said, I felt the scales dropping from my eyes. The scam cell was a tightly controlled group. Their activities were carefully managed and there was a reason for their every action; in other words, no meaningless activity was allowed. It was rationalized to the extent that it made one feel good. But what was the reason for forming such a highly controlled organization? The answer: come what may, the cell's location must not be discovered by the police.

This group was controlled for just one reason: not to be

---

[7] *Oreore sagi*; similar to what is called the "grandparent scam."

unmasked. Actually, several measures to avoid discovery were included in my description above of a morning at a scam cell.

For example, the players, on their way from the station to the office, did not exchange greetings and each one kept to himself; this was done so that if one was arrested, it would not lead to all the others being arrested as well. While the cell was in operation they were strictly forbidden from exchanging contact information; if it were discovered that they did things like going out drinking together after work, they would be punished severely. It was a cell principle that even revealing one's real name was forbidden; everyone was called by their work alias.

Further, their staid businessman looks were for the purpose of preventing the people they passed by on their way to work or the other tenants of the building from thinking that suspicious people were gathering here; the cell had a strict dress code similar to those for junior and senior high school students. Everything was specified: hair length and color, the color of their suits, the style of their shoes, even the quality of their wristwatches. It goes without saying that youthful fashions such as piercings and accessories were strictly forbidden. Those who had tattoos[8] were not allowed to take off their suit jackets or roll up their shirt sleeves, even in midsummer. The code was so strict that they even were made to wear false glasses if their glance was too piercing, and any scars that stood out had to be covered with a bandage.

There also were detailed defenses in case the cell actually was raided by the police. For example, pressing the elevator button with a knuckle was because if they pressed the floor button with their finger it would leave a fingerprint that could subsequently be used as data in an investigation. Some among them who had police records with their fingerprints on file coated their fingertips with glue to form a thin, light film.

The check of personal belongings was to discover anything that might reveal a person's identity in case the

---

[8] In Japanese society, tattoos (*irezumi*) are associated with gangsters.

police raided the cell and found them. After all, if nothing like that was brought to the cell in the first place, if by chance a raid should occur, all the players had to do was escape with just the clothes on their backs. Likewise, commuting by one's own car or motorbike was forbidden. Commuting by car requires a driver's license but even if one didn't bring the license into the cell itself there is the risk that a security camera in the area will capture an image linking a player to his license plate number.

To make double sure, this supervision is not limited to the time players are at work in the cell because it is just during the players' free time that they are likely to act in ways that may come to the police's attention. This is the reason for the strange incantation of "the nine prohibitions" mentioned above. These nine articles cover exactly the points in the players' private lives that might arouse suspicions in the police or people around them and lead to an undercover investigation. The purpose of reciting them every morning is to firmly instill them as regular habits.

For example, the first item, "liquor," is a rule to avoid situations in which a player indiscreetly spends large amounts of money earned from fraud indulging in extravagant entertainment at bars or cabarets, making people wonder what this youngster's source of income is. Using drugs of course is out of the question; people who have a history of drug abuse are not allowed in the cell at all. Further, telling a woman what you do for a living is likely to form the seed of a rumor that "that guy is a scam artist." Gambling and fighting can lead to being questioned by the police about fraud through the practice of arrest for an unrelated offence;[9] engaging in any other illegal sidelines also has the risk of arrest for an unrelated offence.

---

[9] *Bekken taiho*: arrest for an unrelated offense. This is a practice in which a person is arrested for a minor offence to give the police an opportunity to interrogate the suspect concerning a more serious crime. See Cleary, W. B. (1991). The law of criminal procedure in contemporary Japan (1). *The Hokkaido Law Review,* 41(3), 312-234, pp. 288–287. https://eprints.lib.hokudai.ac.jp/dspace/bitstream/2115/16774/1/41(3)_p312-234.pdf

Attire too can lead even family members to wonder why one is so well-heeled. Banks, the final item, means that one should never deposit money earned by fraud in a bank account under your own name. Obviously, if a young person who is not engaged in any legitimate business and who is not paying taxes suddenly deposits a large amount of money, the tax office will become suspicious and this will lead to police investigations, so the rule is to hide your money in cash someplace. In these ways the players thoroughly hide their private lives from the eyes of suspicion.

What should one think? Through interviewing these scammers, I have gone beyond amazement and am mostly just struck with admiration.

Of course, not all cells are as extreme as this one. Among them are obviously disreputable-looking young men working ad hoc, and there are cases in which the players are arrested a few weeks after the cell starts operations. However, these are just second-rate cells. In the case of a first-class fraud organization with thorough management skills as described above, the same way of doing things is adopted throughout; in other words, it uses a template.

The rapid pace of the fraud industry's development is amazing. Losses from the "It's me" scam increased tremendously in 2003. Eleven years have passed since then but in fact, in just three or four years since 2003 this organization management template appeared. I have described the situation in those years in my book *Furikomi hanzai kessha* [Bank transfer crime fraternities] (Takarajima -sha, 2013) but I would like to consider here just who is the target of their scams.

The targets of their scams are not chosen at random. Many years have passed since the people able to achieve this high level of management developed this scam. It goes without saying that they have considered thoroughly and deeply just who the fraud would work on most efficiently and from whom they could take the most money. In Japan today, who is holding the most cash and is the easiest to cheat? Inevitably, the ones who are targeted are the elderly.

1.3 The remarkable evolution of scams targeting the elderly

It is not too much to say that in fact fraud organizations have evolved, specializing with the aim of deceiving the elderly and taking their money. Among them, the ones who have evolved most rapidly are the name list brokers who provide information on the targets to the cells as "subcontractors" of the fraud organizations. Scammers today do not simply make phone calls at random. Invariably there is a name list with phone numbers to call.

However, in 2003-2004, the first years of the "It's me" scam, they did use the inefficient door-to-door-like method of calling up people who appeared to be elderly using the white- and yellow-page phone directories published by NTT (Nippon Telegraph and Telephone Corporation). According to players active at that time, they highlighted names written with a single character or names written in *hiragana* or *katakana*,[10] these being characteristic of elderly women, to make their calls.

This actually led to a certain amount of damage from fraud. There is a good chance that the fact that a women's name is listed in the telephone directory means that she is an elderly woman whose spouse has already died. An elderly woman living alone, without children or others with whom she could consult, is the ideal target. With the spirit of "anyone can succeed given enough tries," the scammers kept on making calls but certain basic information was lacking: Did that person have the ability to pay?

This marked the appearance of the name list brokers. Of course, these were not the usual name list brokers. For most people the term "name list broker" refers to the companies that provide the name lists for so-called DM (direct marketing), the various direct mail envelopes that

---

[10] *Hiragana* and *katakana* are the two syllabaries used in Japanese; female names written in this style were popular in the past

are sent to one's home out of the blue. These come from name list brokers serving as advertising agencies that compile lists of people with various attributes and in some cases act as a proxy for everything from producing the direct mail to mailing it. However, the companies that participate in the world of fraud are only counterfeits of the DM name list brokers.

These companies basically compile name lists of previous buyers (victims) of unscrupulous door-to-door sales and fraudulent mail-order sales, operating secretly in the background to support fraudulent sales methods and crimes. These lists of victims' names are called "sucker lists"; people who, for example, have been high pressured into buying very expensive bedding, or have been pestered day after day into buying expensive water purifiers or having their houses remodeled to withstand earthquakes, or by recommendations for futures trading; the names of such victims wind up on these lists. There are also rumors that these name lists have leaked to even newspaper distribution agencies and victims have been made to subscribe to all the national newspapers.

In short, people who have a certain amount of money and find it difficult to refuse will be defeated by pushiness, time and again, by whatever method. Based on that assumption, these sucker lists are constantly being compiled.

Naturally, the scam cells too target these people who cannot resist pushiness. At first these sucker lists were sold through name list brokers to fraud organizations as they were. But that was only the first step of the first step.

The needs of the scam cells are clear. They want lists of people who are easy to deceive, and just elderly people who have the most money. To meet this demand, the name list brokers developed new tactics. Originally, the usual direct mail name list brokers have large numbers of name lists of elderly people as described above. However, in most cases these listed only name, address, and telephone number. A few might have the date of birth as well but that was all. To supplement this, the shady name list brokers began to contact directly the elderly persons on those lists and collect additional information; they then provided these enhanced lists to the fraud organizations. This additional information represented the name list brokers' advance into the fraud business.

1.4 The actual situation of fraudulent surveys targeting the elderly

First, how did they get the information? The means is what are called "fraudulent surveys." For example, what would happen if someone called your house pretending to be the national census, a crime-prevention survey by the local police, or a survey by the local welfare office checking up on the living conditions and safety of the elderly?

One quiet afternoon the phone rings at the home of an elderly person. The caller is a male speaking quietly. "I'm very sorry to disturb you but this is the Life Safety Section of the *** Police Station. To protect the elderly from crime we would like to ask a few questions and confirm your safety. Can I take a few moments of your time?"

"Oh, really? Thank you so much for your trouble." One can just see the elderly person bowing her head at the telephone. This is the method of fraudulent surveys.

What the caller does is to assume the name of some public organization and claim that he is calling to confirm the safety of elderly persons and carry out a social welfare survey. The usual reaction is to respond naively. If a target seems doubtful at this point, she is rather likely to be ridiculed as a suspicious old crank. But there is real danger here.

These surveys are what the scam cells call preliminary surveys; they are carried out by the name list brokers themselves, or there are cases in which a retired scam player sets up as a preliminary surveyor and is commissioned to carry out these surveys. By these surveys, they find out everything the fraud organization needs to know. For example:

- Is her residence owned or rented?
- Does she live alone or with family?
- If her spouse is deceased, the spouse's name and date of

death.

- If she lives alone, how often does she contact her children or other relatives?
- Is she concerned about her finances? Besides property and securities, how much cash does she have on hand?
- Does she keep her financial assets in cash at home or in a bank?
- Is there someone close by with whom she can consult when uneasy?
- Is she using any home nursing care? If so, how frequently and what kind?
- Is she concerned about her health? Is her decision-making ability deteriorating? Does she feel in danger of becoming senile?
- Has she been a victim of fraudulent sales practices?
- What is the name, address, contact information, place of employment, and the division employed in of a child or other person to be contacted in case of emergency?

This is really detailed personal information; the preliminary surveyor, using the name of an official organization, and with a show of concern for the victim, draws out this information. This is very bad because it is just the elderly with a variety of worries that are the targets of fraud.

Further, a person with experience in the preliminary survey business told me that, in the worst cases, the elderly who are most likely to become the targets of scams answer politely to all of those questions and on top of that they talk for a long time and spontaneously reveal things that weren't even asked for. This is the psychology of elderly people who live alone with feelings of isolation and unease, which is just what the preliminary surveyor hopes for. Further, this act of making a telephone survey assuming the name of a public organization does not in itself immediately become the object of a sweeping police investigation. As the man with experience in making these preliminary surveys said, "It's just a polite crank call."

What value do the scam cells find in the information obtained by these surveys, and what sort of targets do they concentrate on? First, the most important prerequisite is whether the targets have money to pay to the scammers. Formerly, when remittance scams in which the victims were made to pay though banks were the main method, the condition was whether the victim had sufficient savings. However, as financial institutions adopted anti-scam measures, the method of collecting money in a scam today has changed to handing over the cash in person or sending it by parcel delivery service or registered parcel post, so the best targets are those who keep their money in cash at home. In any case, there is no use attempting to scam elderly people who do not have any money.

Second, the cells seek those who live alone and who are isolated, having little contact either with children or neighbors. Even better is information indicating that they previously have been victims of fraudulent sales schemes, but with no one to consult with have just cried themselves to sleep. When an experienced player handles these preliminary surveys, he can pick out instantly the type of person that can be cheated from her responses and tone of voice.

Finally, the icing on the cake is detailed information on children and relatives living elsewhere. If the survey reaches this far, the scenario becomes possible. Among special fraud crimes, the most typical is the "It's me" scam; let's take as an example the most basic type, the "three roles" scam scenario.

1.5 "Hello, hello, it's Kensuke..."

The time is nine a.m. Having arrived at the office, three players who have completed the check of personal belongings and the morning chant form a team at a table. Then Dokugawa, the manager of this cell, gently turns on a radio cassette player. But what comes from the speakers is neither music nor a radio program. What comes pounding out of the speakers is background noise suggesting a crowd, and then the sounds of a train.

"The commuter express bound for Kawagoe is now arriving on track three. For your safety, please stand behind the white line."

These are the familiar sounds of a train station. However, in addition, for some reason, telephones and other office sounds are mixed in.

In this now noisy office one young player, looking tense, picks up the cell phone. In front of him is a name list in a file. He reads the detailed information that has been written there, takes a deep breath, and begins to dial.

An elderly woman answers the phone.

"Eh…Hello? It's Kensuke… Ah…. I…."

The young player, his shoulders drooped, changes his voice, sounding exactly like an ill person on the verge of death. Is the name he used, Kensuke, the name of the son of the woman who answered the phone? Hearing these clearly abnormal words, the woman, flustered, replies, "Kensuke? Is it Kensuke? What's the matter?" but the young player just sighs into the phone.

Now a somewhat older player takes the phone from the first player and speaks. "Hello? Is this the mother of Moriguchi Kensuke? My name is Sugiyama. I am with the Railway Police Unit at the Omiya Station on the JR Saikyo Line. Today at approximately 8:30 a.m., Kensuke has been arrested on suspicion of groping a high school girl on the train and is now being questioned…"

Just then, the third member of this group of three players grabs the phone from the man playing Sugiyama of the Railway Police Unit and begins mouthing off in a loud, threatening voice:

"Hey! I'm the father of the high school girl your son groped! She called me crying her heart out and I rushed over. Damn it! Look what your son has done!"

This man plays the role of father of the groper's victim. He and the man playing the role of railway policeman take turns grabbing the phone from each other, impressing the details on the woman at the other end of the line.

"Please, sir, that's not the way to speak…"

"Bug off! Would you be calm if it was your daughter that was treated like this?"

"Just hold on! Carry on like this and you'll be arrested

too!"

With an expression saying, "The hell with you!" the man playing the role of father gives the table a loud kick. Of course, the sound of the table breaking can be heard by the woman at the other end of the line.

The man playing the railway policeman again takes the lead on the phone.

"I apologize for the disorder. Concerning Kensuke, the normal procedure would be for me to take him to the police station in this jurisdiction, from where he would be taken to a detention center to await trial. However, he has admitted his guilt 100% and if possible, he would like to negotiate an out-of-court settlement. This is a civil matter so the police would not be involved…"

Here again the victim's father grabs the phone.

"Out-of-court settlement! Don't talk rubbish! How did you raise this kid? This is your fault! First, apologize as his parent! My daughter was bullied all through junior high and stopped going to school, and now finally she recovered and could start high school, so this couldn't have happened at a worse time! Your son has ruined my daughter's life! This is not a matter of money! Are you listening to me? Your son works for the Higashi Nihon Bank, right? He works for that big company and on top of that he's a section chief, right? But he's just a piece of trash, your son! I'll splash his name and his company's name and the fact that he's a groper all over the Internet! And I'll plaster flyers nonstop in front of his company and his clients too!"

His shoulders squared and red in the face, the man playing the father's role continues to shout angrily and gets so excited he breaks into a sweat. Now the man playing the railway policeman, wearing the same determined expression, again grabs the phone.

"Are you just going to keep saying the same thing over and over? Now, Kensuke's mother? The other party again has become agitated. I apologize for that. Concerning what I said earlier, would it be all right if I have a subordinate from the victim's father's company go to your house

Preying on the Elderly

now so you could give him a provisional amount for the out-of-court settlement? Kensuke will have to provide a written statement later but the out-of-court settlement is a civil matter so the police will no longer be involved. After he provides the written statement, he will be free to go to work."

Again the father, gasping for breath, seizes the phone. "Listen, old lady! It's my daughter's life! I'm a parent too so I'll make you pay up till it hurts! Don't think you can solve this with small change! Fork out everything you have!"

1.6 The logistics of the three-man team scam

This is a three-man team scenario; among those, the method using the railway policeman is standard. The three -man team consists of three players acting separate roles; this is a theatre-type scam with roles for a policeman, etc. The players seem almost to be actors. How is the victim pressured psychologically by this scenario? Let's look at the players' aim more closely.

First, the basic outline is that a family member of the targeted elderly person must have done some serious harm to someone. Three roles are allotted to the three players: the perpetrator, who is the target's family member (Kensuke), the person who has been harmed by that family member (the father of the girl who was groped), and a third, disinterested party (the railway policeman).

The player taking the son's role must just call the target and say his name; he hardly has to speak at all. Rather, the longer he talks, the more the target may come to doubt that he is really her son; his role is to keep on crying in a hoarse voice, flustered at the fact that he has been arrested for groping, quaking at the thought of losing his social standing. He cannot bear the weight of his own crime and cannot even speak normally.

The second role, that of the victim, is called the "hot tempered role." He is furious at being a victim of this crime and presses the target in a threatening voice. His resentment will not be appeased by just a legal trial; he insists on a private settlement. He performs with anger, conveying that his true feeling is that he won't settle this just with money.

The player in the role of the railway policeman is to help the target who is being subjected to this anger and pressure. He is the only one who is calm. He soothes the abrasive victim, saying that everything can be arranged by an out-of-court settlement. If it comes to an arrest, the damage to the young man's reputation will be incalculable. He kindly proposes an out-of-court settlement to avoid the son's being arrested and losing his job.

If things were left as they were, the young man would be arrested and taken to jail; he would be absent from work and if the facts got out, he would be fired, and after that, a prison sentence. However, if the mother prepares the out-of-court settlement money and makes the settlement now, this social damage can be avoided. Which should she choose? The target is forced to make that decision.

This three-man team scenario has a great many variations just by changing the roles. With the son who had an illicit affair with a colleague's wife and got her pregnant, the colleague himself, and the lawyer who is trying to mediate, the target is given the choice of an out-of-court settlement or a lawsuit that will get the son fired. Or the son who has embezzled money from his firm, the company president who says that he will have to dishonor a bill because of this embezzlement, and the manager who wants to avoid dishonoring the bill by borrowing temporarily the necessary funds from the employee's family. Or the son who has caused a traffic accident, the husband of a pregnant woman who had a miscarriage because of the collision, and the lawyer that he called to the scene. In the basic logistics of all of these scams, the common aspect is the scam cell players' teamwork. The point is that the two main players, excluding the son's role, take turns on the phone one after the other, putting the target into a state of confusion. The three players' bravo performance presents the target with a desperate situation and at the same time offers a helping hand, so that she is placed in a situation of begging "Let me pay the money!" "Please help my boy!"

1.7 Scenarios of frauds made possible by preliminary surveys

We might call this performance outstanding but in fact at the dawn of the three-man team scenario and the "It's me!" scam, things were more rudimentary. The above scenario was made possible only because detailed information about the victim's family was provided to the scammers by name list sellers and preliminary surveyors. Thanks to this, the "It's me!" scam, which had been considered for a time by the fraud industry as old hat, has seen a revival.

For example, in the above narrative, the scammer taking the son's role uses the target's son's actual name when making the phone call. He doesn't say just "It's me, it's me!" If he knows the son's wife's name, he can say, in a tearful voice, "I don't want Misako to find out about this."

Further, the name of the son's company and his position was included in the father's script. This makes the script sound more realistic and makes the target think that no scammer could possibly know that much about her family. Knowing such detailed information as the son's company and section makes it possible to improve the scenario: instead of the Railway Police, the mediator is the son's superior in the same section at work, on whom the boy always relies. This too is possible because of the more detailed information provided by preliminary surveys.,

Knowing the target's financial situation makes it possible to propose an amount for the out-of-court settlement that the target can pay. If the scammers know that the target keeps cash at home, and also know that there is no one close by that the target can talk things over with, then they can set a time limit and put the target in a panic: "We're going to send a motorcycle express service now to your address to pick up the money" or "Please put the money in a Japan Post Letter Pack envelope and send it to this address within 30 minutes." The point is to put the target in a state of confusion and impair her decision-making ability.

In this way the name lists, enhanced with additional information, become a tool to make the scam pattern more realistic, but that is not the only frightening thing. By using these name lists that have been enhanced by the preliminary surveyors, scam players say that they can get the money even if the target half suspects that this story is a scam or even if she is certain that it is a fraud. How can this be?

1.8 Making full use of the victim's psychology

As the scam cell players make dozens of these scam phone calls every day, they become well versed in the targeted victims' psychology. As a result, this unbelievable logic is created.

For example, even if the elderly person who has become the target thinks, "There's something funny here. Could this be a scam?" the man on the phone playing the victim is clamoring in a rage. Further, the callers are saying things that imply that they know not only her own address but her son's address, workplace, position in his company, her grandchildren's names, and even the names of the schools they go to. In such a situation, what sort of mental state will the targeted elderly person fall into?

If the target decides that this is a scam and hangs up the phone, then if by chance this is not a scam her son will lose his social position. But supposing, suspecting a scam, she calls the police; if this turns out not to be a scam there will be no chance for an out-of-court settlement and her son's situation will become even worse.

In many cases the targeted victim is defeated by this mental turmoil and easily has her money taken, but the players' goal is something more than that.

When the targeted victim thinks that this certainly is a scam call, a certain type of target will be overwhelmed by an even greater concern than that her son's social standing might be ruined. That is because when receiving this call based on a name list enhanced with personal information, the target understands from what is said on the phone that the scammers have obtained important personal information about her family. This leads her to worry that she, her children, or her grandchildren might become victims of the scammer's reprisals.

"They might get angry and set my house on fire, or take revenge by killing my children or grandchildren! If they carry out scams like this, probably murder is nothing to them! What shall I do?"

Actually, it is for this reason that at the scam cells it is said that "the hot-tempered role makes the scam." In this way, the player taking the hot-tempered role continues to vent his exasperation in an extremely loud and forceful voice at the target, who has fallen into unease, and this has a multiplier effect.

For example, aren't there people who, when they hear in the street a man's audacious voice raised in argument, become frightened even though it has no connection to them? This is because they have no tolerance for or strength to resist violence. When the preliminary surveyor has experience as a scam player, he can imbue his speech with a tinge of coercion and gauge the target's reaction.

For a target to whose name in the enhanced name list has been added the notation "cannot resist violence," the hot-tempered player's speech will cause her to anticipate violence and to fear being subject to violent reprisals if she decides that this is a scam and hangs up.

In fact, it is 99% certain that scam players will not commit reprisals directly on the targets. The crime of fraud does not involve physical harm to the victim because the aim is to take the money by a performance over the telephone without meeting the target in person. To cause physical harm to the target is like "assisting the police with their investigations"; scammers immediately lose interest in a target whom they decide is not going to give up any money.

If the target thought through the situation calmly, she

would realize this but, tortured by unease, she is swayed greatly by the thought that "if there is even a one percent chance of a reprisal I would rather pay the money so that I never get a call like this again."

This is why the players believe that they can get the money even if the target suspects that it is a scam. This is not fraud, it is extortion and blackmail, but to escape completely from the fear of reprisals from those who hold the enhanced name list, one would have to have body-guards at one's own home, one son's home and work-place, and even for the grandchildren, or else just move away.

However, there are limits to what the target can do. After all, the psychology of wanting to pay and then run away is no different from the psychology of dealing with a high-pressure salesperson, who has parked himself in the foyer, by buying an expensive product just to get him to leave. This victim's psychology is well-known in the world of shady businesses. For this reason, the players do not miss a chance at such victims. Proof of this is a situation the scam players call "fever."

The "fever" situation is a "second helping" in which money is continuously taken two or three times from the target after she has been victimized the first time, yielding even greater amounts. The origin of the word is probably from its use in pachinko to mean a string of consecutive jackpots.

An expert player is well aware that the target on the other end of the phone line may be speaking calmly but, in her heart, has fallen into a state of extreme confusion out of fear. If the player decides that the target has surrendered to the fear of violence, he will plan several "second helpings," launching a variety of scams one after another. The victim, out of fear of reprisals, neither contacts the police or consults with anyone but continues to pay and pay.

According to a *bantō* of a fraud organization who has managed several players, there was a target who paid out nine times in succession without ever contacting the police, so the players involved grossed 60 million yen in just two weeks. For those players, this target was truly a pachinko machine that yielded a string of continuous jackpots.

What do you think about this? Interviewing fraud victims, I felt keenly that their statements that "I was stupid to fall for a scam" were themselves foolish. They shouldn't blame themselves. The scammers are very well trained. The fraud organizations are strictly managed, high-level groups, the players practice thoroughly the techniques for their roles, and the name lists that support them have rapidly improved in quality; for these reasons, the losses from fraud do not decrease.

Further, the above is just the logistics of the "It's me!" scam, the simplest among the many special fraud crimes, and among them what might be called the classic three-role-type scenario. Even this method, which has been ridiculed at the fraud cells as a "traditional performance art," causes people to think "How can I avoid being harmed by this group?"

However, the situation is getting even worse. As I wrote above, in fact there are fraud cells of varying grades but from about 2013 a new movement began at the so-called "main" fraud organizations, with their skilled players and enhanced name lists. That was a trend toward producing name lists in-house and enhancing their contents. Just what are these?

Please recall the producers of mailing lists for direct mail mentioned above. Originally, in Japan, numerous mailing lists are circulating as legal products to support a variety of businesses. Probably the leakage of Benesse's customer data is fresh in many people's minds.

1.9 What happens to leaked customer data

The leakage of customer data from Benesse Corp. occurred when the personal data of about 23 million customers were copied by a systems engineer and sold to mailing list brokers; this event shocked society. It was reported that the data were sold and resold, eventually arriving in the sales promotion lists of companies such as ECC, a major operator of English conversation schools, and JustSystems, a leading technology firm.

Actually, as far as the fraud groups are concerned, the data on Benesse's customers is a name list of parents with children of school age; it cannot be repurposed to a name list of elderly persons whom the scammers want to target. However, recently the actual situation is that name lists produced by direct mail mailing list brokers legally and openly are being bought up by underground mailing list brokers with connections to fraud.

A mailing list broker connected to fraud that I interviewed immediately after the Benesse incident had this to say.

"Scams based on name lists that direct mail mailing list brokers produce for sale existed from the early days of the 'It's me' scam. For example, around 2004–2005, the 'It's me!' scam targeted the families of teachers and doctors. For doctors, name lists of medical school students were in circulation, for teachers at public schools there were name lists of those who were transferred in April each year;[11] the scam was based on these. Of course, now the scams focus on the elderly, and the direct mail firms have masses of data related to elderly people. For example, there are name lists of people who invest in real estate, of people who retire from government service or large corporations, of people who own condominiums, and even of people who belong to country clubs, and so on. There's nothing to it. Some of these have now been digitized so for example if you combine the data from these with those from a previous sucker list and sort it, what will happen? You'll soon find the names that appear in both lists; they are the people who are highly likely to be taken in. Given this kind of data, the screening can be done in an instant."

Readers who use the Internet might just search the lists of name lists held by direct mail brokers. You will soon find name lists one after the other: "wealthy retirees," "airline company retirees," "resort club members,"

---

[11] The Japanese school year begins in April.

"purchasers of expensive jewelry," etc., etc. It will make you wonder where they collected this data and if it really is permissible to commercialize this sort of information.

Even an amateur can easily do what the name list brokers call "screening." Take for example a person whose name is listed on a mailing list of people with significant assets, and whose name appears also on a list of people who requested information about nursing homes. This person has two attributes: she has money, but she is already harboring anxiety about her mobility and decision-making ability. Doesn't that make her a target for scams?

Of course, most of the mailing lists used by direct mail brokers are fairly basic, containing only name, date of birth, telephone number, and address; as such, they cannot be used by the scammers as they are. However, as stated above, by employing preliminary surveys, a highly enhanced name list can be produced.

At present, beneath the surface of the fraud industry, information is being bought up from direct mail mailing list brokers on a large scale to make such enhanced name lists. The man who worked as a scam-affiliated mailing list broker told me, "The success rate for scams using just name lists of elderly people is about 0.25% but with enhanced name lists the success rate can be as much as 40%." Setting aside the reliability of these figures, this is truly frightening!

1.10 You could be a scam victim in your old age!

Furthermore, a big change in the relationship between these underground name list brokers and the fraud groups has been taking place from last year. The following is a statement from an active *bantō* of a fraud group concerning this situation: "What makes the information valuable is how deep it goes. When I was just a junior player we used to buy raw name lists (names without any additional information) from a two-bit name list broker for three yen per name, but when we made the call some old lady would start yelling 'this is the twelfth time this month I've gotten the same kind of call!' You could see how many other cells already had used the same data: it'd been copied so many times you could hardly read the print. Compared to those, the ones that have been polished up (enhanced) by a pro name broker give big returns but for that reason they're expensive. The best name list is one that hasn't been used by any other cell but the name broker knows it's the best so you have to shell out one or two million yen to get your hands on it. That'll come to 10% of your take."

Is this a display of self-confidence by the name list broker? In fact, as far as I have seen in my investigations, the people carrying out the scams are basically of a different age group from the name list brokers. The scammers are in their 20s with the oldest at most in their 40s but the name list brokers are in their late 30s or older, with some in their 60s, in other words, people who have lived in the world of corrupt businesses as "born and bred underground operators." They are very troublesome, sometimes playing the role of the experienced elder, or sometimes taking advantage of the scammers.

"I don't know how many times I felt like killing them. After all, on the cell side, it would be quicker if former players get together and form a preliminary survey group (a group that enhances the data of a direct mail broker's name list by fake surveys); also, people with experience as players know things that the name list brokers don't. For example, how gaga the mark is, is she the type to give in to threats, is she likely to be scammed even if she isn't gaga—someone with scam experience can tell these kinds of things."

This is the trend towards producing name lists in-house. In other words, at present, the scam groups tend to do the work formerly done by underground name list brokers. There are two important reasons behind this trend.

First, it is very costly to buy the name lists that form the basis of the scam name lists from ordinary direct mail name list brokers, and then have them enhanced by a preliminary survey group. Further, among the typical underground name list brokers are those who are not very particular about the quality of their name lists, and there are brokers who cannot come up with the seed money to enhance the lists. Given this situation, it makes more sense for fraud gangs that have the capital to make the name lists themselves.

The second reason lies in the change in the scammers' methods of collecting money. Formerly, as the term "remittance scam" shows, it was most common to collect the money in the scam though bank accounts but because various regulations have been strengthened recently there has been a switch to cash handovers in person. The "bagman" [*ukeko*], (the person who collects the money) visits the victim's residence or arranges to meet her someplace and collects the money directly. However, this method has a very high risk of the bagman's being arrested on the spot compared to the "withdrawer" [*dashiko*] type, in which the scammer simply goes to an ATM to withdraw the money.

The fraud gang *bantō* quoted above had this to say: "Originally, the bagmen were considered expendable but the main cause of being arrested was the use of a cheap name list. That's because somebody who has gotten 12 scam calls will have notified the police. A recruiter who uses a cheap name list to send out bagmen will say 'I've got no more bullets (people)' and blame it on the name list, so the people at the top will have to squeeze the name list brokers. But scam gangs want to have as little trouble as possible, so the reliability of the name lists is a matter of life or death. For the cells too, the level of the name list brokers that the *bantō* are connected with affects their own take, so they've got to do something. So they say, 'Let's make our own!' So the trend is not to depend on the old name list brokers anymore."

Therefore, the present trend is that the name lists used by scam cells are ones that the main fraud organizations obtain of wealthy elderly people held by legitimate direct mail name list brokers and have enhanced by a separate preliminary survey group. Everything is for the purpose of taking large amounts in the most efficient way; this trend causes us to predict a truly frightening future because these name lists that the main fraud organizations obtain from direct mail name list brokers also contain the names of people presently in their 50s and 60s who have significant assets.

"People of this age are still OK mentally but five or ten years later their brains will turn to mush and they'll become gaga. The thing about a name list is that once it gets into circulation it's used to the max. Just a short while ago (1960s – 1980s) there was the wasteland sales scam; that had a follow-up scam where you would tell the guy who bought the worthless land that 'we found a buyer for your land and we can sell it if you pay for surveying and leveling the ground.' Aren't the name lists from that time still floating around? The point is that a list of names you collect today will still be around ten or twenty years from now."

In other words, name lists are being enhanced more and more. The gangs are thinking that these special fraud crimes will still be going on more than ten years from now. The candidates for becoming the targets of future scams are naturally wealthy people who spend and invest; name lists of such people are in circulation among direct mail name list brokers to a surprising extent. In such a situation, these above-board name list brokers are perfectly legal, and provide an important tool for sales promotion in a great variety of businesses.

We can predict that it will be quite difficult to bring this under legal regulation in a short time. Even people who are now still of working age could become victims of fraud in their old age after retirement.

Chapter 2

Why doesn't preying on the elderly decrease? The true character of Fraud, Inc.

2.1 Why doesn't preying on the elderly decrease?

In Chapter 1, I described how advanced the techniques are that fraud gangs use to target the elderly, showing that we should never say just that those who get tricked are stupid. In fact, scam gangs using such advanced techniques are just a small minority; many gangs are just copycats of these gangs and the copycat gangs are soon arrested. Even so, we still cannot be at ease.

"If things remain as they are, the rampancy not only of scams but of organized crimes against the elderly (i.e., preying on the elderly) will never be stopped." After repeated investigations of young offenders who have perpetrated various crimes, this is one thing the author can assert.

I have introduced here a variety of scam methods so I probably could make a scam prevention manual but that would be completely trivial and meaningless. Rather, crime prevention information about the basic scam tricks already is covered sufficiently by the publications of the police, consumer affairs centers, and so on. We can expect that just reading that information will have a considerable effect in preventing these crimes. However, even if crime prevention is introduced, the storm of preying on the elderly will never subside. Why? The reason is that in the very brief time since the rapid increase in incidents of the "It's me!" scam, which is said to have begun in 2003, preying on the elderly has become consummately organized. Let's go one step further and look at that organization as a whole, its various levels, and the power relationships among those levels.

2.2 Company profile of Fraud, Inc.

The present-day scam cells, which have developed to a high degree, are managed almost as if they were companies. It is by no means just because they have offices and the staff members working there wear suits and commute to work like salaried employees. The structure of these highly evolved organizations in fact is very like a corporation. First, let's look at the company profile of Fraud, Inc.

The main business of Fraud, Inc. is to swindle most efficiently the largest amount of money possible from elderly people who have large assets. Their management principle is to take as much profit as possible without any of the employees or higher echelons being arrested. Therefore, their organizational structure is rationalized thoroughly to accomplish this simple aim.

The organizational structure looks like this. First, if this is a corporation, there must be stockholders who supply the working capital, and Fraud, Inc. too has "stockholders" who supply the funds needed to open the scam cells. These people are called "backers" or "owners." These words are in the plural because Fraud, Inc. has several backers. In fact, capital from multiple sources is invested in Fraud, Inc., with several backers riding on the backer who provides the most capital, like an actual largest shareholder.

Fraud, Inc. uses this money from the backers to start its business and invest in plant and equipment by opening scam cells; part of the profits is then returned to the backers in the form of dividends in proportion to their investment. The position of CEO, who brings all of this together, is called a *bantō*. The *bantō* gathers the money from the backers and prepares the equipment needed for the scam (offices, phones for contacting the targets, sucker lists, scam scenarios) and then opens the actual scam cell locations. One *bantō* can manage only about three or four cells. In cases of opening more cells with funds from the same group of backers, several *bantō* join together. In a usual company, this is called the branch office system;

each *bantō* then holds the position of branch office manager.

However, the *bantō* are quite autocratic. In addition to planning the opening of a cell, the *bantō*'s work covers a wide area, including personnel matters, serving as a communications hub, managing the cell's "anti-crime" measures (i.e., avoiding the police), taking care of the accounts, and even "social services." Under the *bantō* rank are the cells, as described in Chapter One; the *bantō* makes the round of the cells, discussing with cell managers such as Dokugawa operational plans (such as the choice of the most effective scam scenario at that time).

The top ranks of this organization consist of the backers as stockholders and the *bantō* as autocratic CEOs. Now let's look at the details of how a new scam cell is set up.

2.3 The process of opening a scam cell

Mr. Kato, a youth of 28, is a *bantō* who manages several cells that use the "It's me!" scam method, which has been called the "one-shot" type in the scam world. His hair is combed back neatly, and his complexion is dark. His eyebrows show determination and his eyes glitter as if he is always thinking about something. He is so composed that his looks do not betray his age. Has the intensity of the time he has spent made him that way?

One evening, Kato is summoned to attend a dinner party given by the main backer of the scam cells that Kato manages. The venue is a famous grilled meat restaurant with private rooms for meetings that caters to those who need a place to meet, from Tokyo gangsters (yakuza) to politicians. The word "party" tells us that other high-ranking and powerful hoodlums will be in attendance. What in the world do they want with Kato?

Basically, the main backer and Kato have tried hard to meet as infrequently as possible. There were discussions at the time they opened the cells concerning financing and the ways that they would obtain the various tools needed for the scam, but Kato does not make detailed reports. Some backers of other cells insist on close contact out of fear of losing their capital, but Kato has only contempt for such backers because those who try to maintain close ties with the *bantō* who are connected to the actual cells are too much off their guard for an illegal business.

Kato nervously enters the restaurant room, bows deeply, and unhesitatingly takes the lowest ranking seat. The whole company, wearing stern expressions, offers him expensive meat with ingratiating smiles.

"Ah, here's Kato. Sorry for the sudden summons. Your profits have been climbing recently, haven't they? Don't be shy. Dig into the meat!"

"Thanks. I will!"

Unnecessary speech is forbidden. Kato is acquainted only with the backer; he has no idea who the other men are, maybe gang leaders, or men who also have invested money in the cells he controls. To ask would be rude.

"You're young but you have a lot of spirit!"

There were tough-looking men who said things like this, offering him a drink, but there were others who studiously ignored him as if he was of no importance at all; formerly, that was the usual way.

Originally, in the outlaw society in which gangsters were the main backers, there was a history in which scams were seen as shameful temporary acts. Eight years ago, when Kato was 20 years old and just starting to work on the lowest rungs of the fraud organization, the situation was such that by just inviting a scammer to this kind of party, the gangster who was managing the party would be told, "We can't let this kind of trash in here!"

But in just a few years, the way scammers were treated changed. On the one hand, criminals were suffering a continuous closing off of various sources of funds by the unrelenting pressure of the police, and had to change their way of thinking; it was also the flexibility of the gangsters who constantly had to change their situation to keep up with the times.

"For gangsters, he's a valuable youth because he will sacrifice himself for the bosses and because he brings in money. We have to treat well guys like Kato who bring in money."

Even so, why was Kato suddenly summoned in front of this group? It goes without saying that he was unable to refuse the drinks offered to him by these toughs. Even as he emptied glass after glass of the sake offered to him until his stomach was full, Kato couldn't get drunk in the least.

Finally, sometime later, his main backer spoke to him in a low voice. "Sorry about that. They're old-timers after all. Guys who are going to invest in you would toss in the trash a kid who loses his head after a few drinks." It seems that the hoodlums gathered here are considering putting money in the cells that Kato is managing as a *bantō*. By their appearance, they were all in their 40s or 50s; some were missing half the fingers on their left hand.[12] Even if they were not registered members of a crime syndicate, they certainly did not look like upright citizens.

"I can't get drunk in this situation," Kato responded in the same low voice. The backer then got right to the point. "I thought so. Now, this is what I wanted to talk to you about. How do you lay in the tools?"

"Tools?" Kato was puzzled at the unexpected question.

"Tools" are the telephones needed for the scams. Originally, as the term "remittance scam" shows, the money was collected in bank accounts so at that time the tools included the "mouth" or the "board" (slang for "bank account") but recently this method is no longer common; the usual way now is to collect the money in person, so the word "tool" refers mainly to phones.

"For the tools, a tool guy (also call a 'suitcase' guy; a dealer specializing in the sale of illegal tools) is involved. You can get a shuffled SIM for about 50,000 yen. Two big tool guys were involved with a bond fraud that was ex-

---

12 "*Yubitsume* is the ritualistic self-amputation of the proximal digits at the distal interphalangeal joint (DIP) among members of the Japanese mafia, or yakuza. This practice of self-mutilation is done as a sign of apology for making a mistake deemed punishable by higher-ranking members or violating the code of the yakuza." Bosmia, A. N., Griessenauer, C. J., & Tubbs, R. S. (2014). Yubitsume: Ritualistic self-amputation of proximal digits among the Yakuza. *Journal of Injury & Violence Research, 6*(2), 54–56. https://doi.org/ 10.5249/ jivr.v6i2.489

posed last year, and took off, so I had a really tough time getting hold of some."

The "shuffled SIM" is a SIM card for a cell phone account that belongs to a third party. If the scammers use an account in the name of a perfect stranger with absolutely no connection to them, after that account is used in a scam and the account holder is investigated, it will not find its way back to the scam organization. The tool dealer gathers "account players" who will become cell phone account holders and has them open as many cell phone accounts as each cell phone company will allow one individual to open; then the dealer sells the SIM cards to scam organizations and others. When the tool dealer buys the account from these account holders, and when he sells them to the scam gangs, it is also his job to put a "cushion" (a third party who has no connection with this) in between so no connection can be made from the holder of the account used in the scam to the scam group itself.

However, it is often the case with these contracts that the holder does not make the first payment after taking out the contract, so the cell phone companies soon suspend the service. The scammers call the victims within this time span, but this means they have only limited use of an account costing 50,000 yen. An "It's me!" scam cell of average size will use up 50 or 60 shuffled cell phone accounts between the time it opens and closes down. This cost, the biggest "investment in plant and equipment," is borne by the backers who are the stockholders in the scam organization.

"Oh?" Kato's reply was curt, but the backer smirked. It seemed that something was up.

"Let me ask you. Can you take on six more 'It's me!' scam cells in half a year?"

"Six! Is that on top of the cells I'm running now?"

"Oh. Is that too much?"

"No, I can't say that it's too much but…"

This was really unreasonable. Six "It's me!" scam cells require gathering a minimum of 36 players to make the calls, and 54 would be ideal.

This assumes a nine-player system per cell. This has been Kato's policy. In the case of the three-role "It's me!" scam with one team of three members, if there is only one team in a cell, the cell's atmosphere will tend to become slack, however outstanding the cell manager who has brought these players together is. However, if there are two teams, the cell's atmosphere will tighten up and a spirit of competition will emerge. If there are three teams, the manager can make an expert team composed of highly experienced players that can guide the other two teams while competing for results; further, the expert players can work closely with the newcomer teams and advise them.

In any case, however many teams are placed in one cell, the expenses associated with that location, such as office rent and utilities charges, remain the same, so it is obvious that if the number of teams in one cell increases, the profit ratio goes up. On the other hand, it is a very big job to find so many players; further, it would be impossible for Kato to manage that many cells by himself. This proposal is really a big headache for Kato.

"Why this proposal all of a sudden?" When Kato asked this question, the backer's voice became even softer.

"I've got a new source of tools!"

"Is this new source OK? They're not reshuffles?"

"Listen, you, don't be stupid!" The backer seemed to lose his temper slightly, but it was reasonable for Kato to be worried. "Reshuffles" are cell phone accounts where some time has passed since the original account holder signed the contract, so that the remaining possible use time has become very short, or the person who had employed that account holder to establish the account already has been arrested. They are sold by a scam tool dealer to scam the scammers, but if one is pressured to use such an inferior phone account by a backer, even if no business results are produced, the ones who suffer the damage are *bantō* like Kato and the players in the cells who cannot make any money.

"It's OK. I'll tell you my source. The guy is a dummy

loan shark who specializes in tools. The story is that he's holding a list of one or two hundred names of washouts (people who couldn't pass the screening for an illegal loan) who'll gladly do it."

"Dummy loan shark?"

"The setup is that he lends a small amount, say 50,000 yen, to people who have taken out multiple loans without any ability to repay them in the first place, and then has them pay it back with the fee he gives them for taking out phone contracts. If he can round up ten people who are not blacklisted (people who are in arrears in their payments and cannot open new cell phone contracts), he can get more than one hundred contracts for an investment of 500,000 yen. If we spread these around, we won't run out of tools for a while."

Clearly, this is a source of new shuffled cell phone accounts.

Kato himself has heard from loan sharks he knows personally that recently there has been an increase in the number of young people who, after graduating from university, have not been able to find employment and start running to loan sharks. Students, particularly male students, who cannot find employment are in a situation in which, far from having no collateral, they have minus collateral; they cannot possibly get a loan even from a loan shark. If so, it would be a waste to ignore those young people who have actually approached a loan shark but have been turned down. He had recently been approached by people asking, "Isn't there any way I can get some money?" That might be a way to get players.

It seems that the backer's detailed talk had stimulated Kato's underground businessman's spirit.

"Is this deal already in the works?"

"Not yet, because the shuffles are still raw. First I have to confirm that the cells are up and running."

This was silent pressure. Shuffled contracts become useless shortly after they are taken out so if the scam cells were not ready at the point when the contracts were obtained, the one who bought the contracts would suffer

a big loss. This would mean a loss of profits for the backers. On the other hand, if there were not enough contracts
when Kato had assembled the cell players, Kato would be
the one who sustained a big loss.

But the backer was still smiling. There was yet another
layer here.

"Just listen up. It's not just the tools. The name list is a
category one list with 3,000 names. They've all been
scrubbed [enhanced] so it's expensive, but I'll put up the
surety. The guy wanted a 15% use charge, but we settled
for 10%."

"Really?"

This was a different order of magnitude. A "category
one" name list is one that has never been used in a scam
before. One with 3,000 names that has been enhanced is a
gold mine, Kato thought. However, the dealer who actually produced and sold this name list would be very bullish
in providing it to the scammers, considering that an enhanced number one name list is a treasured item.

The "surety" is the money paid to the dealer whether
the name list is used in a scam or not. Dealers often do
not take surety for a used name list, but a high-quality
name list can go for millions of yen. On the other hand,
the "use charge" is the percentage of the profits paid each
time to the name list dealer when a scam using that name
list is successful.

Should Kato really go along with this? The plan immediately turned his thinking around completely, but the pend-
ing question was whether it was feasible to gather so many
people. At Kato's cells, the system was to pay the players a
minimum daily wage. If he assembled many players but
didn't have enough tools or the name lists were worthless,
it would be a matter of life or death to Kato himself.

"Is it really OK? If we get ten percent hits from 3,000
names and get a million yen from each hit, that comes to
300 million yen. If by bad luck the hits are only one percent, I'll have to cover the loss, won't I? Speaking frankly,
it'd very tough to train as many as 50 newcomers. Paying
them an allowance of 200,000 yen during two months of

training comes to ten million yen. Recently my transportation expenses for going around to the cells comes to 20,000 yen per day so if the cells operate for two months, that's two million yen... And if we're short-handed, I'll have to find replacements somewhere."

"Listen, you. Don't talk so cheap. The name list dealer is saying this will yield 20 percent hits, so by your count that's a 600 million take. This item is the real deal. It's OK to use sub-*bantō* so let's do this. This time we'll even provide the "box name." If you don't want to do it, I'll get someone else." The short-tempered backer, looking at Kato vacillating over this grand proposal, seems to have run out of patience.

In this connection, the "box name" is the actual leaseholder of the office used as a scam cell. Naturally, as a measure against exposure, they need the name of a third person who has absolutely no connection to the backers, the *bantō*, or the cell players, and this too is a big part of the expense of operating a cell.

The cost for using someone's name might be 200,000 yen per month or a lump payment of 200,000 or 300,000 yen. However, after all, a scam cell frequently changes its location to prevent exposure; if a cell operating for two months changes location three times, six cells will need a total of 18 leaseholders. Further, organizations that have things firmly locked up even go so far as to have a different person rent the office next to the one being used as the cell; here they store cash and the items they need such as cell phones and name lists. They get or replace these items when necessary using the veranda, and they promptly dispose of documents, memos, etc. in a shredder placed in this office.

In such a situation, if the amount paid to the person whose name is used is a lump sum of 200,000, a simple calculation gives a total of 3,600,000 yen. If the neighboring office is rented as well, this doubles to 7,200,000 yen. The backer is saying that he will pay for this.

Hearing that the backer has a good deal of confidence in the new route for tools and the 3,000-item name list,

Kato too seems about to make up his mind. "I see. It's really a gamble for someone like me. Can you give me tomorrow to think it over?"

"No, I need your answer straight after lunch tomorrow. If you're in, I need the time because there's a lot I have to take care of." This shows the dynamics between the backer, who is the shareholder and investor, and the *bantō*, who is the CEO.

The backer, using his extensive personal connections, will gather the name lists and tools, the office leaseholders, and in some cases even the recruiter who will dispatch the players to the scam cells, and supply the appropriate capital. However, he will have absolutely no connection with the operation of the scam cells; he just "introduces" the tools and the money, and afterwards looks on from a distance and collect his dividends.

On the other hand, from the *bantō*'s point of view, this is a big gamble. Even in case of a failure, the backers surely will come to collect the principle. In fact, the *bantō* would like to provide everything though his own resources and connections but in fact he is no match for the backers, whose connections are far-reaching. Recently, there has been an increase in cases in which *bantō* establish cells with their own capital and become the backers of the cells that they operate, but even so, they cannot compete with backers, who operate on a different order of magnitude; their position with respect to the backers is such that it is difficult from the beginning to refuse a project that they have been told to take on.

"Let me think it over" means "I'll do it." And once he accepts, he cannot withdraw later.

When the meeting is over, Kato leaves immediately for a nearby business hotel where he had reserved a room. He takes out pencil and paper to calculate just how much things will cost under the conditions of the backer's plan. With his gut filled with liquor he starts phoning his contacts. There is no time to rest. Intensely busy days start tomorrow.

2.4 Name lists are the ingredients, players are the chefs

What do you think? I wrote above that scam cells are very like a corporation, but the most similar company organization is that of a chain restaurant: a shop with nine staff members, including the manager; a company president who controls several shops; and the stockholders (investors). Considering the number of staff members in one shop and the number of shops one *bantō* can cover, thinking of the scale of a community-oriented pub chain makes it very easy to understand. We can just replace the name lists with the ingredients, the cell phones with disposable kitchen items, and the players in the cell who make the calls with the chefs and service staff.

Kato is a company president who is suddenly directed to expand operations in the fraud organization, which resembles a corporation. The first people he contacts as a matter of course are the cell managers who are running the cells he has at present. Kato himself had the experience of being promoted from player to cell manager and then rising to become CEO (*bantō*). Further, this project would be impossible to carry out if he did not use a sub-*bantō* who could oversee cells along with himself. Unhesitatingly he calls his most trusted cell manager.

"Sorry to call you so late. Is it OK to talk?"

"Somebody get picked up?"

The one who answered the midnight phone call in a nervous voice was Dokugawa, a cell manager who might be called Kato's right-hand man. He was a powerhouse who had up to now turned an *ipponbako* (scamming 100 million yen during the brief two or three months an "It's me" scam cell stays open) five times. In fact, Dokugawa at 32 was four years older than Kato but the "seniority-based wage system" and use of polite language was reversed by the influence of the company president – branch manager relationship.

Dokugawa had had a shady career: a loan shark player in his teens, in his twenties he operated as a real estate investment agent and seminar lecturer. He opened a sex shop with the money that he had earned, but the man that he had entrusted with the money to run it ran away with the proceeds and one of the girls who worked there. When he asked a gangster whom he knew to get him back, the gangster, who had a high opinion of Dokugawa's smooth line for scams as a former real estate investment agent and seminar lecturer, suggested that he become a scam player as a stopgap job.

Being that kind of talented performer, Dokugawa's reaction after hearing the details naturally was hesitant.

"Six new cells? Can we really do that? It would be a waste to give such an expensive name list to inexperienced players. You've got to have very smooth-talking pros."

"That's so. At present, how many players have you given business phones to?"

"20 at best. Including the ones who are in the cell I'm running now it won't come to 30."

"Business phones" are different from the shuffled phones used to make the scam calls; these are cell phones used for communication between players and cell managers, among *bantō*, backers, and cell managers, with the cash collectors, etc.; they are usually prepaid cell phones bought by a third person with no connection to the others. These are similar to company cell phones or internal lines; unlike the shuffled phones, the phone bills for these are paid regularly and they are used for a long time.

"30? You're great! I'm happy to be doing business with you. So, if there are 20 that we can actually use among them, we have to gather 30 more. I'll spread the word to the other cell managers; how would that be?"

"How many managers are you in contact with?"

"Four, including you."

"So, if you've got to run six cells, you need to set up two more cell managers."

In spite of himself, Kato was struck dumb. It is not too much to say that the take from a scam depends on the cell managers. From Kato's point of view, Dokugawa, who has given business phones to more than 20 experienced players, was his strongest subordinate. Having several such cell managers and being able to handle any proposal, however big, is, in other words, the measurement of how big the *bantō* is.

"If worse comes to worse, I could manage a cell while being *bantō*," Kato said, sounding slightly desperate, but Dokugawa replied,

"Ha ha. You're joking, aren't you?" His voice sounded somewhat cold.

"Yes, it was a joke."

That was only natural. For a *bantō* to be involved in a scam cell as a manager was strictly forbidden in large fraud organizations.

What is in force here is the principle of compartmentalization. The rank-and-file players at a scam cell may know that there is a *bantō* but do not have much contact with him. In some cases, they do not even know his name and there are even cells where the compartmentalization is so thorough that the players believe that the cell manager is the top and do not even know of the existence of the *bantō* as company president. What this means is that if by chance a rank-and-file player betrays the cell to the police, the investigation would not reach as far as the *bantō*. As far as the backers above the *bantō* are concerned, they exist above the clouds; rank-and-file players have never met them and do not even know of their existence, so it is almost certain that the backers will never be unmasked, at least by following personal connections. It is for this reason that a *bantō* must never take on an additional role as a cell manager.

However, seeing that Kato was desperate, Dokugawa seemed willing to act.

"Joking aside, what should we do? There are two guys among my players who might be OK to promote to cell manager."

"Really? What are they like?"

"They're 23 years old, still kids."

"Hmm."

"Please say something. I'll vouch for them. If you don't

want to trust them at first, I'll be sub-*bantō* and watch over their cells."

Kato's thinking again took a full turn. Nothing would suit Kato better than if the talented Dokugawa would become a sub-*bantō*. In fact, Kato, who had worked very hard, moving slowly up the rungs, and had finally reached the rank of *bantō*, was becoming slightly fed up with this work. How long would he have to keep struggling in this position? He had been thinking this way for a long time.

Certainly, it was true that once one became a *bantō*, as long as you weren't arrested, you could earn in a few years as much money as a salaried worker made in a lifetime, but it was as if your life was in the backers' hands. You could get out, but only up to the rank of cell manager. However, for Kato, who at present was a *bantō*, if he could train Dokugawa as his successor, this was a chance to quit this work, escape from the backers' shackles, and finally return to a normal life.

"I get that you're vouching for them, but 23-year-olds, I wonder…. Anyway, to be blunt, to work as a sub-*bantō* while managing a cell is probably a lot harder than just working as a *bantō*. I could help you with the bookkeeping, though…. If you work as sub-*bantō*, you'll be noticed by the guys above and that will lead to your being asked to be a *bantō*. You won't be able to escape from this work."

"But I'll do it! Having come this far, I wouldn't be a man if I didn't go for it," he said decisively. Hearing this, Kato made his decision as well because those words echoed the decision that he had resolved on when he himself was chosen to be *bantō*.

2.5 Backers never get arrested

Fraud organizations are similar to corporations; they have the same sense of scale as a community-oriented pub chain. Given this, if this business was not a scam, the people here could be thought of as zealous workers. Faced with this unreasonable demand from management to expand his business, how will CEO Kato cope? Is it possible for him to make this project succeed and at the same time train Dokugawa as his successor and safely take the next step?

However, here I want to return to the main theme of this book. Why will preying on the elderly never cease? One important reason is in this story. Stating it point-blank, it is very simple: preying on the elderly will never cease because the fraud system has been organized so that the backers, who are the highest level, will almost never be caught.

Let us review this company's organization chart again. First, the basic structure of Fraud, Inc. consists of several shareholders (backers), CEOs (*bantō*), the cell managers, and the players operating under them in each cell. In addition, there are external cooperating businesses that support the fraud organization's business from outside; these include the name list brokers, the tool dealers, and recently the "collection agencies," which have no connection to Fraud, Inc. Collection agencies are independent groups that manage the bagmen who approach the scam victims and collect the money directly from them.

Underlying this, as stated above, is the principle of compartmentalization. First, it is impossible for the arrest of a cell player to lead to the arrest of a backer at the top because the rank-and-file players do not know even of the backers' existence. Second, if Kato were to fall into the hands of the police, the chances that he would give up the backers to the police are zero. This aspect is greatly different from a typical corporation.

For example, when corruption reaching the entire upper management of a typical enterprise is revealed, would a manager sacrifice himself to protect them? Probably not. But in the fraud organization the *bantō* will certainly protect the backers. What is operating here is not an economic principle but the "principle of evil."

For the *bantō* to give the backers up to the police would the same as putting an end to his life. Naturally he would no longer be able to live in that world and probably would have to spend the rest of his life in fear of retaliation. Here certainly is the dynamics of evil involving violence.

On the other hand, if the *bantō* continues to confess that he is the one at the top of the organization and acts as a shield to prevent the chain arrest of the backers, that is seen as an accomplishment and a proof of his reliability.

It is frequently the case that the *bantō*'s share in a fraud organization is half of the net profit after expenses have been deducted from the scam take, but considering that there are several backers, in fact it is the *bantō* who gets the largest share from the take of any one cell. In other words, even if he is arrested and given a long sentence, if he has managed to hide a certain amount of wealth, after he leaves prison his assets and his reliability in the underworld society are guaranteed.

The idea of "sacrificing oneself," that is, "sacrificing oneself for the group to which one belongs," is much more highly valued in the underworld than in society in general; this dynamic is at work here.

2.6 In the unlikely event a cell is exposed

Now, one more. In this book, I have used frequently the expression "in the unlikely event a cell is exposed...." The sense of the event being unlikely is very real in the scam cells.

They operate under the assumption that it is impossible for the police to raid a cell. Rather it is just because of this assumption that whenever there is news that another fraud organization's cells have been exposed, the scam world is thrown into confusion. "How did that happen? We thought that it was absolutely impossible for a cell to be exposed! How did the police ever reach that cell?" With such feelings, they rush around wildly gathering information. This is a scam cell's typical perception.

Why do they believe so strongly that a scam cell is absolutely safe? The basis for that belief is in the most unmitigated aspect of the principle of compartmentalization described above. It is the compartmentalization of the flow of money.

Fraud, Inc. uses collection agencies as external cooperating companies. In the past there was a collection section within Fraud, Inc. itself but at present it is now common to commission external collection groups to collect money.

This is only natural because both formerly and now the easiest person for the police to arrest among all those involved in the scam business is the one whose job is to collect the money. The method has changed from collection by "withdrawers" using bank transfers in the past to the main methods of collection today, which are by bagmen who collect the money directly from the victim, or by the shipment method using parcel delivery services or parcel post; in any case, if the mark senses a scam and notifies the police, and the police lie in wait, the collector will be summarily arrested. These collectors are the soldiers on the front line of the battlefield and bear the brunt of the attack.

However, even if they are arrested, the main fraud organization couldn't care less. Of course, they probably regret the loss of the profits that they had hoped to gain; the arrest of the collector was careless, but the investigation will not reach the main fraud organization because there are five layers of protection.

The first layer is "silence." Basically, the collectors have been trained so that even if they are arrested by the police, they just keep saying "I was asked to do it by a stranger," or "a foreigner asked me to do it," or just keep silent. By doing so, even if they are convicted and sentenced, they have a firm promise from above that they will be provided for after they get out.

Recently the bagmen have been getting younger and there are even juveniles among them, so it is common for a first offence not to involve prison time. Even in the case of adults, they were not the main actors in the scam, so it is difficult to prosecute them for a fraud crime with a heavy sentence. Considering that they get off with a light sentence, isn't it natural that they would prioritize the network for their livelihood and work in the future, and remain silent?

The second layer of protection is cutting the individual's

personal connections. In the first place, in a collection agency, the rank-and-file bagmen are not personal acquaintances of the agency chief; they have met face to face only a few times and there are cases in which they do not know even a telephone number by which he can be reached.

Even if they knew the phone number, that number would just be a "business" phone like those used by the main fraud organization, so even if a bagman, under severe interrogation by the police, revealed that he was asked by an agency chief, considering that he does not know that chief's identity, such as his real name and address, the police would not be able to find their way to that chief.

The third layer of protection is cutting personal contacts within the organization itself. If the bagmen are in fact the collection agency chief's local younger colleagues, then the chief himself may be arrested, but beyond him the police investigation hits a big wall.

First, the line of command for a scam collection goes from the *bantō* or the cell manager to the collection agency chief, and then from him to the bagmen who actually make the collection, but the communications among them are done only by voice using shuffled or business cell phones. This is because sending directions by mail would leave a history that could be used as evidence; further, when the *bantō* or cell manager phones the collection orders they do it from places far from their own cells to make it impossible to deduce the location of the scam cells from the base station data that is contained in the cell phone call history.

Next are the ones that really foil a police investigation.

When the collection agency chief receives the cash from the bagman, he uses means such as leaving it in a toilet stall, or under a park bench, or passing it from one car's window to another to establish one cushion. Further, the money flows finally from the agency chief to the *bantō* but naturally this is not done in person but by using a messenger who has no connection to either organization or by using a coin locker or a private post office box. Further, the messengers are instructed that when carrying the cash to change taxis and trains frequently and even to stay in crowded places such as busy stores and station platforms.

What does this all mean? Suppose that the police follow the flow of the money. The police are informed of a scam, and by using a stakeout, observe the bagman receive the cash from the victim and let him go on, based on the principle of following the money, not the person; even so, they cannot possibly follow the movement of the money. Unless they insert an ultra-micro GPS tracking transmitter into the cash, they cannot trace it from the collection agency until its arrival at the scam cell.

The strength of this third layer of protection depends on the *bantō*'s leadership; however, at present (autumn, 2014) it is said that four cushions are standard. That is to say, the structure is that if the collection agency is A, B gets the cash from it, C from B, D from C, and finally the money arrives at Fraud, Inc. from D. This structure has become so common that at Fraud, Inc. sites, the collection agencies are actually called "A" or "A agency." If we count each cushion as a separate layer of protection, Fraud, Inc. is protected by six or seven layers.

2.7 I assert: preying on the elderly will never cease

I assert again: Preying on the elderly will never cease.

I believe that the scammers have created a stupendous organization. Preying on the elderly has become an industry that supports this large number of people. The starting points for police investigations are those who collect the money from the victims and the account holders of the cell phones, but here too, concerning both connections among people and the flow of money, a thoroughgoing principle of compartmentalization thwarts an investigation.

On the other hand, this also can be called a thorough principle of cutting off the tip, like cutting off a lizard's tail in stages. And that tail will grow back again and again. In the fraud business, the ones who most often sacrifice themselves for their masters (i.e., get arrested) are the bagmen, but I found in the early stage of my investigation that the men given this job were those who had to earn money no matter what. In addition to people deeply in debt, people with disabilities, and ex-cons, there even were those who had heavy medical expenses from serious illnesses, or were male prostitutes. These people who desperately need money to live until tomorrow are given the task of collecting the money, the dangerous front line of preying on the elderly.

At present, with the shift in the means of collection to the type in which a bagman meets the victim directly, the age of the people involved is becoming younger. If the perpetrator is a youth with no previous record and does not hold a leading position in the scam, it is difficult to prosecute him for a serious offense; further, to a young tough in his teens, being arrested for a scam just makes him feel important. On the other hand, there are even macho-type bagmen who, when accosted by the police, can knock over a robust policeman and run away.

In any case, the bagmen are infinitely replaceable, and the hands of the police never reach the backers; this top level has the capital to set up scams for preying on the elderly again and again. Given the existence of this structure, whether the means are scams or something else, crimes targeting the elderly using every means possible will continue.

For the police to eradicate this, they would have to arrest the *bantō*, cell managers, and players for more serious crimes compared to the bagmen, and furthermore make them think that this kind of work does not pay. They would have to arrest the *bantō*, who is the head of the scam cells, and make a deal with the prosecutors to assure the *bantō*'s safety in the future, and then get from him information about the backers to eliminate them.

However, the reality is just the opposite. A raid on a scam cell is a rare event; examples of persons of the backer class being arrested can be counted on the fingers of one hand, even though ten years have passed since remittance scams became a social problem. This is the perception of the people involved.

This is why preying on the elderly will never cease. The one thing that we might hope for is that the players on the ground, who are supposed to be thoroughly managed, will make light of the possibility that the police will discover their cell and be off guard, or, considering the amount of money involved, thumb their noses at the world at large and show off in their private life. You might think that that might happen but that would be a big mistake.

As I interviewed the people involved in these scams on the ground, what continued to surprise me was not the brilliance of their techniques, measures for avoiding exposure, and organization theories, but rather the outstanding qualities of the cell players and the *bantō* themselves, their humanity, their backgrounds, and the strictness of the beliefs they held.

The *bantō* and cell managers belong to the "lost generation"; beneath them are those disparaged by the term "relaxed generation," and further, the youngest stratum belongs to the "enlightened generation."[13] In any event, they are the young people who have been made into a "disappointing generation" within companies and elsewhere by the generations above them.

However, the young scammers that I met in my investigations were not like that. Were they really brought up within that generational view? Were these kids really

---

[13] "Japanese workers currently [2018] in their mid-30s to mid-40s are known collectively as the 'lost generation,' or the generation of the 'employment ice age.' They started job hunting after the economic bubble collapsed. As Japan slipped deeper into a serious financial crisis in the late 1990s, companies tightened up on hiring new employees to keep the ones they already had." Okutsu, A. & Anzai, A. (2018, October 2). "Lost generation" haunts Japan, Abe and the BOJ. *Nikkei Asia.* https://asia.nikkei.com/Spotlight/Asia-Insight/Lost-generation-haunts-Japan-Abe-and-the-BOJ. The "relaxed" generation educated under the "relaxed education" (*yutori kyōiku*) system, which was designed to reduce cramming and rote learning. They roughly correspond to Millennials. Further, "the 'enlightened' generation is another nickname for today's generation, and it implies that they had only known Japan in its economic decline and had learned not to expect anything, including wealth or even sex." Oi, M. (2015, March 23). Can education change Japan's 'depressed' generation? *BBC News.* http://www.bbc.com/news/business-32013613

brought up in Japan? I have such doubts because the on-the-ground players engaged in preying on the elderly that I met were a group of outstandingly talented people.

In the next chapter I will attempt to answer the question of why preying on the elderly has expanded so much. But I'll give the short answer here. It is because the players are tremendously talented and are very highly motivated, and there is a system in the cells that develops this talent and motivation; further, they have a reason for devoting themselves to preying on the elderly. Lamenting that they have no use for the young people of today, and then becoming victims of scams after retirement, elderly people should read this with a sense of self-reproach.

Chapter 3

Training for preying on the elderly: How one becomes a player

3.1 Training by slapping

In a certain month of 201X, a tenant signed a contract for a multi-purpose building about 40 minutes by train from central Tokyo. The building seems to be a dilapidated ferroconcrete structure about 40 years old, with many vacancies. Several of the mailboxes in the entrance foyer have been sealed with gummed tape. Drops of dirty water from the walls are forming small pools in the first-floor lobby, perhaps because there is no leak prevention on the roof or the verandas.

In one room of that building, at 7:35 a.m. At this time, most salaried workers are still eating breakfast while watching TV, but in one bare office, single-unit student desk-chairs are lined up in rows, and in the rather narrow space between the rows, about 20 men, wearing a variety of street clothing, are standing, wearing tense expressions.

On each desk is a name list printed in fine print on A4 copy paper, one set of business documents in flow chart format, and a cell phone. The young men, standing motionless, stare at the strange scene in front of them.

"You were told at the interview! You think being late from the first day of training is nothing? You shitheads trying to make fun of us?"

Four young men are standing in a row in front of the whiteboard placed at the window of the small office. In the twinkling of an eye their faces are slapped hard.

Smack! At the sound of the violent slaps from an open palm, unlike the usual slapping sound, the expression on the faces of the men standing motionless in the rows between the desks grows even more tense.

The one who was doing the slapping was a well-built man in his 30s, wearing a suit and with a shaven head. Next to him stood a man with his arms folded, also wearing a suit but tall, bearded, and wearing glasses. He turned his hairy face around and appealed to the four young men standing erect and motionless.

"Get it? If you're late again tomorrow, I'll give your ass a beating you won't forget. Those who have a wristwatch, adjust it with the time signal. If you're late by even one second three times, you'll be fired that day. Keep it in mind! Now, go back to your seats."

Holding a hand to their red and swollen cheeks the four young men threaded their way through the narrow space between the desks and returned to their seats. One or two of them wore a somewhat sulky expression but not one of them attempted to sit down without permission. The entire room was tense. Actually, the young men gathered here had answered an ad in a free newspaper and had passed an interview.

"Sales personnel wanted
- *Mainly telephone sales*
- *Take-home pay: ¥300,000 per month*
- *Transportation allowance paid separately"*

A common recruitment text. But the interview had some strange aspects. They were asked in minute detail not only about their present living conditions, financial circumstances, etc., but also about their family structure and relationships, their hobbies and how they spent their free time, whether they were in debt, and, concerning their record of awards and punishments,[14] if they had had any trouble with the police.

They were not told the contents of the work in detail, just that it was a telemarketing job, and this was the first day. Being suddenly slapped for being a few minutes late, being subject to further violence if you were late the next day and fired if you were late three times. Was this what

[14] *Shōbatsureki*: "List of awards and punishments" is a standard section on Japanese CV forms.

was called a "black company"[15]? Standing in front of the whiteboard and facing the young men filled with unease, shaven head and beard-and-glasses stabbed that unease into their hearts.

"You're thinking now deep inside that you wound up in a black company, right? Sorry to say, you've hit it on the head! Anybody who wants to leave, we won't stop them. But let me say this first. From now you're going to get intensive sales training for one month. But we're not the usual black company. The ¥300,000 per month pay mentioned in the ad is really true, and you get that even during training. We'll pay the first installment of ¥100,000 at the end of the first week. The remaining ¥200,000 will be paid at the end of the month. Both in cash. Also, the transportation allowance is paid day by day. Further, after you finish training, the workplace you'll be attached to uses a full commission system so the ones who work hard can easily pull in more than ten million yen a year."

The young men who were listening to this detailed talk about money gulped unconsciously. That was only to be expected because almost all of these men who had passed the interview were currently unemployed and all of them were uneasy about tomorrow's livelihood.

Shaven head looked at his watch and said, "All right, I'm going to wait two minutes. Anybody who wants to quit, leave now. We won't stop you and we'll even give you today's carfare. Start!"

Ten seconds, thirty seconds, one minute, and then two minutes. Nobody said a word and the silence was as if everyone was holding his breath. Not a single person left.

Shaven head and beard-and-glasses exchanged a satisfied look; then, taking a deep breath, shaven head spoke in an even louder voice, shaking the walls of the office. His face, tanned by the sun, became even redder as he scowled at the young men.

"All right, let's begin the training! I'm Koshiba and the

[15] "Black companies" are businesses that exploit their employees by subjecting them to harsh working conditions, such as excessive overtime, tolerating power harassment, etc.

beard is Ushijima. First is voice training, repeat after Ushijima!"

Taking his cue, the bearded Ushijima again took a very deep breath and exhaled without stopping.

"Good morning!"

"G...good morning?" To those who appeared to be hesitant Koshiba yelled in an angry voice, "Can't hear you!"

"Good morning!"

"Good morning!!!"

"Again, louder!"

"Good morning!!!!!"

With over 20 men shouting, "Good morning!" from their guts, the atmosphere of that place became surreal. Overriding that, Ushijima's loud voice rang out.

"Thank you for your assistance!!!"

Just shouting like this, the faces of the men who were repeating were running with sweat.

"Thank you!"

"Thank you!!!

Leading this chorus, Ushijima's face too was covered with sweat.

"Goodbye!"

"Goodbye!!!!"

What would they repeat next? To the men waiting expectantly, Koshiba, relaxing his stern expression, said, "OK, you said 'Goodbye' but nobody's going home yet!" At Koshiba's words, completely opposite from the tightly wound up tension he displayed up to now, everyone was stunned for an instant.

"You can laugh now!" When Ushijima interjected this, a few ripples of laughter could be heard here and there in the room.

"OK! Sit down, everyone. Look at the script that's on your desk. We're starting at 9:00 so you've got exactly one hour to study that from one end to the other. If there is anything you don't understand don't be silent but come up and ask, even about any piddling thing."

Everyone picked up the paper that was on his desk. It

was a sales script for a condo for investment purposes.

Please excuse me for disturbing you with this call. This is XXX of YYY Estates. I am calling to inform you that a new condo for investment purposes, which can be purchased on very favorable terms, is going to be built in your neighborhood.

It was a sales tool in flowchart format; it began with this sales pitch and then the text of what to say next branched out according to what the person at the other end of the line said. However, several faces here and there wore a look of shock when they came to the price of that investment condo; it was no less than 85 million yen. Could anyone possibly sell such a high-priced condo by this kind of dubious telephone sales method?

At this point a young man who had earlier been slapped for being late raised his hand with a question. Perhaps in his early 20s, he was wearing a plain black sweat suit, and his hair was short and slightly bleached; he didn't look like he was ready for work. With narrow eyebrows neatly trimmed and a slight scar on his upper lip, he looked less like an aspirant to a sales job and more like a model for a fashion magazine targeting delinquents. But his glance was piercing.

"Do we have to follow the script exactly?"

"Ah...an eager beaver! What's your name?"

"My name? It's Kurusu."

"Kurusu, is it? You asked a good question. The script is basically just for reference. Just change it as you like to keep the other person on the line."

Change? The young men were puzzled by this, but the one named Kurusu seemed to have another question.

"What do we do when we come to the end of the script?"

At his question, everyone, who had been studying the script, turned to the last page and read it. The script ended like this:

We would like to send you a brochure so please give me your address. Thank you very much. In closing, let me repeat that I am XXX of the sales department. Thank you very much for your time. Goodbye.

Was the end purpose of this sales pitch to send a brochure?

Sneering, the bearded Ushijima replied, "Well, you won't get through it from start to finish so just take it easy. After all, this is just training, just "selling nothing." It says that we will send a brochure but in fact we won't. That's because the investment condo doesn't even exist."

Everyone in the group was surprised at this; Koshiba walked up to Kurusu, who was wearing a shocked expression, and, grabbing him by his lapels, lifted him off of his feet. He was tremendously strong.

"Listen, kid! You think this is a waste of time? All of you, if you can't do this, you won't make any progress. First, you've gotta call and call and keep calling. If you get hung up on, make the next call within five seconds. If I see anyone even put the phone down, I'll give him a thrashing."

When Koshiba dropped Kurusu as if tossing him aside, the atmosphere in the office again became tense. Ushijima continued, piling it on.

"Well, you can't train unless you concentrate. You can have one toilet break every two hours. Other than that, you're not allowed to leave your seat during working hours. Whether shitting or pissing, if you can't hold it in, do it in your pants. Anybody who's got to go, go to the toilet now. Once we start operations, there's no smoking until lunchtime. We'll start in 30 minutes."

The room again returned to silence; in the office could be heard only the slight rustling of the script pages. Several went to the toilet and others, thinking that they couldn't smoke until lunchtime, took a few drags on the narrow veranda; however, everyone quickly returned to their seats and resumed studying the script. Among them, Kurusu, who had been slapped for being late and then grabbed by the lapels, stepped on, and kicked for asking a question, sighed to himself with admiration.

"Dokugawa told me about it to some extent, but this is really something else!"

3.2 Selection by "dummy training"

"Why did preying on the elderly become this big?" Some readers must have thought that I was going to begin with an explanation of that, so felt disappointed by my suddenly going into a description of the mysterious "black" training. However, this is the first step in the training of a scam player. It is a program called "dummy training," which is done for the new recruits.

Originally, men who join a scam cell as players have various backgrounds. First, there are those who are changing jobs from another underground business. A typical example would be a former staff member of a loan-sharking business. Further, there are those who used to work in the sex business as scouts or staff members. In addition, some were scouted while in prison or reform school; there are also former yakuza and those who have delinquent connections, being introduced by someone connected to a cell. In the elite group, there are those who have experience in the operations of shady businesses and those who have risen from the collection agencies, which are the lowest rung of the fraud organization.

These men with a variety of experiences in underworld businesses are the "seed players" among scam player candidates. While participating in training their will to work as a scam player hardens; they are sent directly to an operating cell or assigned to a cell after participating in a training camp where they use scam scenarios from the outset.

However, what about the case mentioned in the previous chapter, in which the *bantō* Kato and the cell manager Dokugawa were ordered by the backer to increase suddenly the number of cells and players? When there are not enough seed players to fill the required positions, this dummy training for new recruits is conducted. Compared to the seed players, who have experience in underworld businesses, they are merely novices.

However intense it becomes, in the end the rule for working in a scam cell is the "dynamic of evil." But a novice has no understanding of what that dynamic is. Until it is known if a person will work out or not, he cannot be told that beyond this training lies a scam enterprise, and a scam scenario cannot suddenly be introduced for training. This is because it would be a disaster if someone should report this to the police on his way home from training.

Consequently, the novices are first given training in worthless empty sales calls in a completely "black" environment while the coaches are observing them to see who has the attributes of a scam player.

Also, among the novices undergoing the dummy training described above, there was one outsider. You can guess who it is: the young man named Kurusu. He was really a plant. He was one of the 23-year-old players mentioned in the previous chapter that Dokugawa suggested to Kato as a cell manager candidate.

The job given to Kurusu was to mix with the novices at the dummy training, deliberately arriving late and being punished, asking questions positively in place of the other novices, and keeping the training session focused. When a currently active player participates in training, he can learn by practical experience the overall know-how for a cell that is required when he is promoted to the rank of cell manager.

Of course, he received from Dokugawa an advance payment of several hundred thousand yen for participating in the training, including a bonus for being hit, but even so, this dummy training went beyond whatever Kurusu had imagined.

3.3 Starting sales training

Sales training started at 9:00 on the dot. All 20+ trainees together put the business cell phones to their ears, and with the name list and script in their hands began to dial. But soon after they had begun Koshiba went to where Kurusu was sitting and hit him on the head with a straw sandal, using all his strength. "Are you just screwing around? I told you that if someone hangs up on you to call the next one within five seconds!"

For a moment, the blood rushed to Kurusu's head even though he knew that that was the part he had to play, but he noticed that Ushijima too was giving a full swing with a straw sandal in front of another desk. Both men were wearing shoes, so it seemed that out of politeness they were using clean sandals reserved for hitting people on the head.

For a currently active player like Kurusu, this empty sales pitch was just nonsense. He had no idea where the name list that they were using came from, and the conversation did not seem to go beyond stating the company name and section. Not only that, the ones answering the phone were often young people living alone; the name list was not targeted at people who might be investors. On top of that, the price of the investment condo was 85 million yen. It was a sales pitch that already was doomed to failure but neither Koshiba nor Ushijima showed any mercy.

"No resting! Don't put down your phone!"

"If the phone keeps ringing that means nobody's home! Hang up and call the next one!"

Shouting abuse and hitting heads here and there with the straw sandals, Koshiba and Ushijima marched through the aisles between the desks. They carried two-liter plastic bottles from which they would refill the plastic cups on each desk when they became empty.

Among the participants were some who soon came to realize that physical strength was needed to conduct telephone sales intensively. Although they were just making phone calls, they were sweating as if they were running up a flight of stairs, and their throats soon became dry.

"Listen up! If one call takes five minutes you can do 36 calls in three hours. If the call log on your phone shows less than that, we'll make you sit kneeling upright this afternoon!"

Because that shouted abuse could be heard over the

phone, the people being called lost whatever interest they might have had and paid no attention to the sales pitch. The trainees soon came to feel that what they were doing was a wasted effort, but the abuse and the straw sandals flew even to those who hunched over, resting their elbows on their desks.

"You scum! Is that the kind of posture for selling with the client right in front of you? If you don't act as if the client was right in front of you, you can't get the right attitude!"

"Do it with the right attitude!! Attitude!"

With this and that, it became almost noon. Everyone felt tense. If they hadn't made 36 calls, they would have to sit kneeling, on top of the other torture. Among them were some who continued to make calls while grimacing and twitching nervously, perhaps holding back the need to go to the toilet. It seemed that the second hand on the wall clock in the office was advancing very slowly out of spite.

At noon on the dot, Ushijima called out, "OK! The morning session's finished. Well done!"

Hearing that, there was not a single person who could reply, "Thank you." Every one of them sighed with relief, looked upward, and unwound their tense bodies.

"Ahh.."

"Oh, no. I can't believe it…"

The room stirred with grumblings that were hardly words. But just then, the whole room was startled again as Ushijima's voice rang out, "OK, we're giving you box lunches so come up and take one. Everybody, go to the john now because lunchtime is 45 minutes."

When they looked they saw that somehow takeout box lunches had been piled up in front of the whiteboard.

What did this mean? It meant that after being worked so hard, they couldn't even go out for lunch but were confined to this office. This was really a "black" training session. The box lunch was nicely arranged and looked rather expensive but everyone, while eating silently, wore expressions as if they were chewing on sand.

There also was a group of men assembled on the veranda who wanted to absorb as much nicotine as possible during the short lunch break. Kurusu was among them.

Damn! I haven't had a smoke since this morning! I really needed this!"

"This is really tough, I think."

Seeing a man who appeared to be in his early 30s sucking on his cigarette with evident pleasure, Kurusu responded in this way. In fact, as a scam cell player, Kurusu himself had had a lot of experience; however, having entered this world through so-called "delinquent connections," the only training he had had was just to be thrust into a working cell and told to "memorize all of this in three days." When he said that this was "tough," he really meant it.

Kurusu and the young man about his own age put their elbows on the veranda railing and spoke seriously.

"Awesome! What a blue sky! Can you believe it? It's only been three hours, but I feel like we've put in three days' worth!"

Several others who were also smoking on the veranda gave sighs of agreement. Just living their daily life, employed at a typical company, they probably would not have been so stressed and forced to concentrate so much in such a short time. It was as if the participants in the training session had been thrown forcibly into an unreal world. They felt that the everyday world that could be seen from the veranda, in which they had lived until just a few hours ago, now seemed strange and distant.

Their respite was brief. From inside the office Koshiba's merciless voice resounded, "We start again in five minutes! Show me that you're eager to work by getting to your desks five minutes early! If somebody says that he has to go to the toilet or something just before the time, I'll kill the bastard!"

When they sat down, they saw that the cellphones they had been gripping tightly all morning looked slightly whitish. They had sweated so much from tension that the salt residue looked white. When Kurusu looked around the room, he saw that three seats were empty. The ones who should have been seated there were not in the office. It seemed that there were some defectors during the three -hour morning session.

"Listen up! This morning three guys asked to quit. As I told you this morning, we won't stop anybody who wants to quit. If anyone wants to quit this afternoon too, feel free."

One again, the pointless sales calling began.

3.4 The loop of calling, talking, and being hung up on

Calling, talking, being hung up on. Calling, talking, being hung up on.

Why was doing just that so painful? Probably many of the participants were thinking so. However, as they repeated this routine over and over again, a change appeared in some of the participants.

At first, they spoke awkwardly, following the script, but gradually their replies came automatically in response to what the other person said. Dialing the phone was a pain but there were some who, when they thought they were going to be hung up on, were already checking the next number on the list. Some even seemed to be working unhurriedly.

Koshiba and Ushijima were carefully observing this change. They would go up to those they saw as smooth talkers and offer suitable advice. "That's the way! Just go on to the next. You don't have to listen to everything they say before you get the picture, right? So don't listen until the end, just talk right over them. It doesn't matter if you interrupt them."

When giving advice, Koshiba, who relentlessly had played the role of the mean coach, bent down in the narrow space between the desks next to the one he was giving advice to. Ushijima too used such a velvety tone when giving advice that he seemed like quite a different person.

"Let's take it one step further. The script ends if the one on the line says he's not interested, right? But some of them just can't hang up on you. That's the kind of jerk who just can't interrupt when someone is talking and hang up. That's your chance, right? So you can just change the script."

"But how should I change it?"

"You figure it out, dummy!" In a flash, Ushijima hit him on the head, but his expression was not angry. "That's what I'd like to say, but after all this is a training session so I'll teach you. For example, suppose he says that he hasn't got the money to invest, so you tell him that he can take out a mortgage without putting anything down. After that, just repeat the same line that you already gave him. If it was you that got such a nuisance call, what would you do?"

"Let me see… It's a real pain in the neck so I'd just tell him to send me the brochure and when it arrived I'd probably just throw it away."

"Sure! Because the point of this sales talk is just to send the brochure. We don't care whether he can raise the money or not. So see if you can take it that far."

The trainee looked as if he understood.

As they all continued to call, one of the trainees called out, "Excuse me!" It was the man whom Koshiba had advised previously.

"What is it?"

"The guy said to send him the brochure and I got his address."

"Good! That's the way to go!"

Koshiba and Ushijima brought their thick palms together and shook hands. Among the trainees, some wore an expression of admiration, while others looked all the more irritated. Just then, Ushijima walked up to the desk of the first successful trainee, pulled some money out of his inner jacket pocket, and threw it on the desk. It was a 5,000-yen bill.

"I didn't mention it before but everyone who gets as far as sending the brochure gets 5,000 yen. There's one hour until four o'clock. After a thirty-minute break, there's another hour and a half to go. If you know what's good for you, you'll kill yourselves trying!"

They were told it was just empty sales but there was a bonus if they succeeded! Further, 5,000 yen was no small amount to them. Everyone checked their watches and focused again on the script and name lists. They were just like the gamblers in a pachinko parlor on the verge of closing, making their last try.

3.5 The aim of training like torture

In the end, three trainees were successful on this first day of training, and each one was given 5,000 yen on the spot. When training finished at six o'clock, everyone was made to stand again and do ten sets of voice training, the same as in the morning, starting with "Good morning!" The announcement that they were finished finally came one hour later. The final words were that anyone who was late for the starting time tomorrow at 7:30 a.m. should expect a punishment worse than today's, and that anyone who thought after today's training that they couldn't keep up from now on, should just not show up.

Released from that abnormal tension, the participants wore a half-relieved expression as they went home along the dark street. Among them, only Kurusu, just pretending to go home, returned to a parking lot near the office where the grinning Koshiba and Ushijima were leaning on a black sedan waiting for him. They had arranged this previously.

"Hey, Kurusu! Good job today! Sorry that we had to slap you around."

"How about it? Let's go get something to eat that you like. How about some grilled meat?"

"Thanks, but my mouth is sore. I wouldn't be able to taste the meat."

"Hah! Is that so? Sorry, sorry."

Both Koshiba and Ushijima were cheerful and laughed a lot, completely different from the way they were during the training.

"You really didn't hold back, the way the flat of your palm came at me. It shook my brain some. On top of that, just spending the whole day on phone sales gave me muscle pains all over my body."

"I know, I know. That's what happens. Spending the whole day on the phone, you get muscle pains."

"Hah!"

Just what kind of people were Koshiba and Ushijima? Originally, Kurusu had been directed by his scam cell manager Dokugawa to participate in this training, but he had never met these two. There was a brief meeting beforehand, but he never dreamed that the training would be this tough.

Ushijima drove them to an *okonomi-yaki* (Japanese savory pancake) chain restaurant on the highway. Sitting in front of the hot iron plate, questions were swirling around in Kurusu's head.

"Have a drink, Kurusu? I'll take you home so drink up."

"Actually, we're not allowed to drink while we're working."

"Is that so! You're a real follower of Dokugawa. He really taught you well!"

"Actually, I have some questions I'm dying to ask you."

"Ask whatever you want!"

His main question was what the purpose of this training that resembled torture was. Of course, if you practice calling to that extent, your jaw probably will become strong (i.e., you'll become a smooth talker) but he had heard from Dokugawa that the training lasts one month. What was the point of continuing this kind of training for so long? First, you rent the office, promise to pay everyone 300,000 yen for the month, and then pay 5,000 yen every time someone succeeds in the dummy sales; won't the cost of this training have to come to a huge amount?

When he flung these questions out freely, both Koshiba and Ushijima laughed uproariously.

"Kurusu, do you really think that this training is going to last one month?"

"Huh?"

"From tomorrow, we're going to slap them around even more, and the script will be even more nonsensical.

They'll learn something from that! So, Ushijima, what shall we do for tomorrow's script?"

"Let's see… How about the one that says, 'Please buy a gravesite for twenty million yen'?"

"Ha, ha. That'll do."

Kurusu was shocked, but Koshiba and Ushijima seemed serious about having them do the gravesite sales tomorrow. However, just then, Koshiba banged his beer mug down on the table and his face took on the domineering expression it had worn during the day's training.

"Listen, Kurusu. There was no intention from the beginning of doing this training for one month. About how many do you think will show up tomorrow?"

"How many? I suppose that there'll be one or two that won't show up."

Hardly giving him time to finish his sentence, Koshiba said, "Too optimistic! The way I see it, we'll lose five. But tomorrow we're going to be tougher, so the count will go down even more the next day. Maybe we'll set the hours from seven am to nine pm."

"If you do that won't everyone quit?" For Kurusu, who had to attend these sessions as a trainer himself, this talk was painful. Ushijima sat silently next to them, cooking the *okonomi-yaki*.

"Listen. It will balance out. We told them that we'd give them the first installment of their pay after a week, right? On top of that, if they get an address, we give them 5,000 yen. The ones with guts will bite at that and hold out for a week. It'll probably come out to about ten."

"Come out?" Kurusu was astonished, so Ushijima explained further.

"Yeah. Well, if it looks like the numbers might drop even more, we might let up a bit at the final stretch. It would be a shame to lose the ones who are really smooth talkers, so to flatter them and get them to stay we can give them some cash."

"Cash…" Gradually Kurusu was coming to understand the concept of this dummy training. These two had no intention from the beginning of keeping most of the trainees.

"Supposing that there are ten guys left who last until the first pay installment at the end of the week. After that some are sure to not show up anymore. Those are the ones who stuck it out to get the first installment. Now, Kurusu, let me ask you a question. What kind of guys are going to get the first installment and still come back for more?"

"Let's see. They're really tough, with plenty of guts... they're smooth talkers and they really want money, right?"

"Right! When you think about it, aren't those just the qualities of a scam player?"

Hearing this, Kurusu, who had a lot of experience in a scam cell, got the point.

"Probably three days after the first installment, or ten days in total, we'll be left with about five or six. Actually, this time Dokugawa asked us to get some people so it looks like he needs to recruit new players. If we have a month, we can run three sessions and pick out 15 more guys just for those cells." Ushijima continued, while skillfully flipping the *okonomi-yaki* over. He was completely different from the way he was during the day.

"I'm confident that the 15 guys who'll be left will have the strength or are in some kind of situation so that they won't quit even when they find out that we're really running a scam. By the way, Kurusu, I haven't told you but among the guys that came to training today, there were some who said at the interview that they didn't have any place to live. So we gave them 20,000 yen for living expenses for the time being and put them all up in rooms in a flophouse that we had ready."

"Flophouse rooms? Did you go that far? It's for sure that all of those guys will stay."

"Don't be stupid. You're being too optimistic again. Even guys as desperate as that will run away if you peel their nails back at training. It's the training that weeds them out."

Deeply interested, Kurusu remained silent. From what they were saying, he saw that the theme of this training was emotional conflict. The coaches' frightening violence showed no mercy, and the trainees were constantly shouted at, as in a harsh black business. They wanted to escape, and the coaches were saying it's OK to leave, but some guys were getting 5,000 yen right in front of their eyes. If you can get 5,000 yen just for succeeding in this empty sales talk, then the 100,000-yen first installment must also be true.

Still more, the flophouse group were those who didn't know if they would be able to eat anything tomorrow or not. However, even these numbers would be pared down. Thoroughly driving the trainees into a corner, they create an emotional conflict in the narrow space between the harsh training and the bonus for success received on the spot. This was the true nature of Koshiba and Ushijima's dummy training.

After thinking for a minute, Kurusu replied, "But there might be somebody who strikes out in a rage. There might be a crazy guy. To tell the truth, even though I knew I was a plant, I was just about ready to boil over."

The two coaches smiled broadly. "Well, well! He's a real golden egg, isn't he? Good thinking! In the end, they'll be made to toe the line, so rather it's those guys who get angry who will be a better fit for the real operation. Kurusu, that's your type, isn't it?"

Kurusu could make no reply. Being just a rank-and-file player, he had never thought of the other players from that point of view. It seemed that there was an awful lot that he could learn from these two. Thinking so, Kurusu felt famished. When he looked he saw that his portion of the *okonomi-yaki* was half scorched. He rapidly put it on his plate and while taking big mouthfuls he renewed his determination.

3.6 What's the meaning of this?!

The training sessions from then were even more severe than Koshiba and Ushijima had promised. On the second day, as Koshiba had predicted, five men failed to show up. Those who were late had their heads pounded constantly throughout the morning session and two of them quit. It was announced that the training session time would be from 7:30 am to 9:00 pm, including the following Saturday. During the noon break one guy even stood up, red in the face, and lashed out at Koshiba. "What's the meaning of this!? Aren't you just hassling us?"

"What? There's no meaning." At Koshiba's seemingly nonsensical reply, the man looked as if he was about to start grinding his teeth.

"I'll say it again. There is no meaning. In fact, the business of telemarketing is just repeating the meaningless."

"I don't get what you're saying at all."

"Well, I'll explain. Just try to imagine. Here is a product that yields a profit of a hundred million yen and there's a team of ten guys doing telemarketing. If everyone makes one hundred calls every day, that's a thousand calls a day, thirty thousand in a month. If 29,999 calls are wasted but there's just one hit, what happens? The month's pay for everyone is ten million yen."

The man that had lashed out looked baffled. However, Kurusu, who had listened to this exchange while continuing to make his pointless calls, understood what was meant. This was very similar to the profit concept at a scam cell.

"Those 29,999 calls are all wasted?" Confirming what Koshiba had said, the man asked another question as if to probe deeper. "Well... Supposing we finish this training successfully, will the products we handle really yield that kind of profit?"

"You bet! If they didn't, this would just be black training!"

The man seemed not to want to persist any further. He just said, "thank you" softly and awkwardly went to pick up a box lunch from those piled up in front of the whiteboard.

Seeing this, Kurusu had the feeling that this place was flowing along a great current. Actually, as a plant, Kurusu had been told to make this complaint: "What's the meaning of this!?" However, somebody who wasn't a plant actually made this complaint, and Koshiba neatly put him down. It was as if it was "pre-established harmony." There was no doubt that the other trainees had absorbed this lesson.

Nine p.m. was the time to finish but that was just the time to finish telephoning. From then there was pronunciation practice again and reading aloud of tomorrow's script.

As the days passed, one would drop out, then two; at the point when everyone would be overwhelmed from exhaustion and lack of sleep, one bottle of a tonic drink costing more than one thousand yen was provided with the box lunch at noon. That made Kurusu laugh to himself but some of the others, when they saw the tonic drink, yelled out their thanks loudly.

Fifteen minutes before starting time in the morning, and five minutes before the noon recess was to end, almost everyone was at their desks. It seemed that the sprouts were beginning to grow among the participants.

3.7 The event on the seventh day of training

In the bare-looking training room, six men, including Kurusu, stood at attention. In stark contrast to the first day, all of them wore suits and showed strained expressions, as if they were different people. Their hair was cut short and their leather shoes were shined. They had survived to the tenth day of training.

It was as Koshiba and Ushijima had predicted. They already had given out the first installment of 100,000 yen on the seventh day, but on that day only nine remained.

Actually, a minor event occurred on the evening of the seventh day. As everyone was returning home with their 100,000 yen, one of them was hit from behind by someone and the envelope with the 100,000 yen that he had just received was taken from him. The victim got a glance at the robber's back and was sure that it was one of the men who had just been training together with him.

Without immediately going to the police he returned to the office where Koshiba immediately gave him another

100,000 yen, adding 20,000 on top of that.

"Well, there are bastards like that around. Good thing that you didn't get injured very much. Do you want to see a doctor?"

"No, I don't have any health insurance."

"I see. Why did you come back here instead of going to the police?"

"Well, somehow…"

Somehow, he had become aware that what lay beyond the training that they had been undergoing would not lead to a typical job.

In any case, the five remaining men (excluding Kurusu) were those who had chosen, for the sake of the remaining 200,000 yen, to put up with this training that was like torture, even if it lasted 20 more days. The suits and leather shoes had been bought at a nearby Don Quijote discount store and a Crown discount shop with 20,000 yen that Koshiba had given them that morning. Looking at their tense faces, Koshiba and Ushijima felt satisfied.

"You've all worked really hard. For ten days up to today, you've done a great job."

"You've worked hard. Congratulations!"

Congratulations? These two coaches had been real devils up to yesterday, so what was this transformation? Originally, they had been told that the training would last one month. These five men had remained just because they had resigned themselves to a repetition of these hellish days for 20 more days. Now their heads were filled with question marks. Even Kurusu, who had not been told of this transformation, had no idea what was coming next.

"Hey, hey! Don't look so puzzled. In any case, the training will continue."

We thought so… They all were pretty much fed up with it but were surprised at Koshiba's next words.

"Actually, today, we're taking a drive. Just think of it as something like a field trip for social studies class."

"The car is waiting in front, so everyone be there in 15 minutes. It's not an excursion but you'd better use the toilet now. Also, from today, smoking is OK. So any of you smokers who want to can light up now." As he said this, Ushijima himself lit up a cigarette, while several of the others released a sigh. It seemed that three of them, including Kurusu, were smokers. Compared to the highly restrictive training, just being able to smoke freely was heaven.

Even so, what in the world did they mean by "taking a drive" and "social studies field trip"? They didn't see what it had to do with sales training.

After they had all gotten in the Toyota Alphard eight-seater minivan that was waiting outside the office build-ing, Ushijima, who was in the driver's seat, immediately entered the expressway.

The Alphard sped along smoothly along the empty highway under clear skies, but where were they going? They crossed the Metropolitan Expressway and went into the suburbs. However, there was no use thinking about it. During the ten days since this training began, none of the participants had been allowed to do things at their own pace; they just bore it with a state of mind as if they had given themselves up to the drifting of the boat they were on. It was not a situation in which they had to think deep-ly about where they were headed.

Perhaps because of the exhaustion they had accumulat-ed, perhaps because they had been released by what Ko-shiba said previously from the tense situation that had lasted so long, some of them fell asleep, snoring slightly. With this and that, after a little less than an hour, Koshi-ba's laid-back voice rang out in the car.

"OK, we're going to arrive soon. Look out of the win-dows, everybody." Being told so, they looked out of the windows only to see just a broad rural landscape. The car left the expressway and entered an area of paddy fields. However, a few minutes later, Ushijimja turned the car towards a mountain of medium height that towered be-yond the fields, and the scenery changed completely.

First of all, the road was better. The rural road that they had been on up to now could hardly be said to have been paved very well and was very bumpy, but as they entered the mountain road the road noise decreased. The road had a clear center line, and neatly trimmed trees lined the road on both sides. Leaving the gently curving road, they saw a valley before them spread out like a different world. Ushijima pulled up by the side of the road, and ordered everyone out.

They were at a golf course. Its broad area was laid out with green grass. Beyond the gate was a large rotary; a magnificent clubhouse in Japanese architectural style rose before them like a super deluxe Japanese inn. The cars parked there also presented a magnificent sight: Audis, Benzes, Jaguars, and Maserati and Porsche convertibles, seemingly vying to be more low-slung than the others, were lined up side by side.

"Any of you guys golfers?" Koshiba asked nonchalantly but all of them said "No!"

"That's what I thought. I've only played a bit myself."

"Listen. You haven't come here today to play golf. In fact, none of us would be allowed inside the gate. But I want you to burn this scene into your memory."

Ushijima, in a penetrating voice, began to talk about the background of this golf course. "This golf course was built in 1988, at the height of the bubble.[16] You all know what the bubble economy was? Anyway, this course uses a membership system. Basically, only members and their guests can play here. By the way, an individual membership costs 30 million yen. The average age of the members is 68." Ushijima's speech flowed smoothly. But what kind of training was this, looking at a golf course from the top of a hill? At this point, none of the trainees, including Kurusu, could figure out what this meant.

"Any thoughts?"

"Er… Its peaceful." These words from one of the trainees in answer to Koshiba's question actually hit the target. A blue sky. The countryside's clear air. The only thing that they could hear was the chirping of birds. The middle-aged men walking on the beautiful grass of the

---

[16] Japan's bubble economy lasted from 1985 to 1990.

huge golf course looked like peas. This was a completely different world from the hellish empty training that they had been forced to do until today.

"Is this land being taken care of just for those few men? Just planting the lawn and keeping it so green must cost a huge amount."

Koshiba and Ushijima seemed a bit surprised at the man who asked this. "Oh, you figured that out, did you? Have you done that kind of work?"

"No, but my old man was a gardener. I was just a kid when he died and the business went bust."

"That so?"

Some of them stretched unconsciously, others cracked their necks, others took deep breaths without realizing it. What was it that the trainees, who were each burning this scene into their memories, felt most strongly? The thing that cut into this time, which resembled a brief respite, was, unsurprisingly, Koshiba's voice.

"OK, get back in the car. We're going to the next stop!"

3.8 Observing people in front of a convenience store

The next objective was just a few minutes from the golf course. Descending the paved road that led from there, they drove toward the countryside. Turning into a straight road, they saw a sign at an intersection saying, "Entrance to XX Industrial Park." This industrial park included companies in the automotive industry, electrical appliances, foodstuffs, and so on; its roads were poorly maintained with deep ruts compared to the roads near the golf course, to say nothing of the roads in the countryside, perhaps because large vehicles roared by unceasingly.

Ushijima pulled the Alphard to a stop in the large parking lot of a convenience store located right in the middle of the industrial park.

"You're all probably getting hungry, right? Sorry, but today's lunch will be a convenience store box lunch."

When the eight of them got out of the car they realized again how huge this parking lot was. This lot was planned so that long tractor trailers could enter just as they were. It

79

was the noon hour so many working people, particularly those in the transport industry, had shown up here and the convenience store was jampacked. Koshiba and Ushijima pushed their way through those workers, bought a shopping basket-full of food for the trainees, and returned to the Alphard.

"There's not much space inside the car so let's eat outside. Next, I haven't told you yet, but this is today's second point."

What were they going to learn in a convenience store's parking lot? Koshiba, wearing a wry smile, understood their doubts. "This is important training so concentrate hard. The object is observing people. Observe carefully the customers who come to this convenience store and burn them into your memory. What kind of people come here, their age, their clothing, their vibes. There's a toilet inside the store so we can take our time here."

In fact, this was a slow and careful course. After they ate lunch, an hour passed, two hours passed but still neither Koshiba or Ushijima gave the signal to finish. They just moved the car to the edge of the parking lot so that it would not be in the way of other vehicles and regularly went to replenish the drinks and so on while the observation of people continued.

Many were drivers. Some were napping in the driver's seat of their trucks that were parked for a long time, perhaps waiting for the time when they could pick up a shipment from one of the near-by factories. Some people in suits who were driving company cars didn't stay for long. Looking busy, they ate while holding a cell phone in one hand, and soon left.

More time passed. Just when some of the trainees, tired from the past week, were beginning to yawn, a large number of men began to shuffle off of a bus that had stopped at the bus stop across from the convenience store. Finally, Koshiba and Ushihima gave orders.

"All right, everybody, check out each individual in that group carefully!"

"See if they have any points in common, what their

average age is, just observe carefully anything you can."

They seemed to be men who are going to work the second shift in the nearby factories. All of them were expressionless; very few walked in a lively manner. And in fact, they had several points in common.

Their plain workpants for some reason were invariably a little short so their white socks showed at the ankles. On their feet they wore plain sneakers, slightly dirty, of the kind sold at bargain counters in ultra-cheap shoe stores. And for some reason they all wore the same cheap backpacks on their backs, and the hair of all those who wore no hat was unkempt or else their hairlines were receding, and the tops of their heads were going bald.

What would their average age have been? From their clothing and demeanor, many were middle-age or older but if you looked at their faces carefully, in fact many of them were young, in their 20s or 30s. Actually, they were men of an indeterminate age.

No sooner than one group had left when another bus arrived with the next batch. Some of them crossed the road and entered the convenience store, but after buying an amount of food that would barely be enough for a snack they rejoined the lethargic line.

Was this group of factory workers what Koshiba and Ushijima wanted to show the trainees? When they looked up at the sky, they saw that the sun was beginning to set.

"OK, that's enough. Let's get back to the office, shall we?" For some reason, the trainees were silent. Until yesterday they had been completely wrung out by the training and today they had unfettered outdoor training. Those who had engaged in some pointless chatter during the morning were all silent. They were enveloped in silence just as if the Alphard were a microbus taking them to a funeral. What change had taken place in their state of mind?

3.9 At the end of drive training

As they returned to the office, certainly doubts were racing around in the heads of the five members who had survived the training to this point. What in the world was the purpose of today's drive training?

They had spent so much time only to visit a golf course and a convenience store parking lot. They felt uneasy because the only instructions they got were to burn the scenes into their memories, so they thought that if they were asked about today's training after returning to the office and gave a wrong answer, they would be slapped around again.

However, Kurusu, the only actual player among them, had pretty much guessed the meaning of today's outdoor training. 'Today's the final weeding out. At last it's over.'

And as Kurusu had predicted, Koshiba and Ushijima, who had entered the office a little after the trainees, wore stern faces. Koshiba, clearing his throat once, began to speak bluntly.

"I'll get right to it without beating around the bush. The training that you've done up to today was all to select staff workers for remittance fraud!"

Instantly the atmosphere in the office froze. At first, the five trainees who were left didn't seem to understand right away. They had been thinking that this training was weird from start to finish, but remittance fraud? Wasn't remittance fraud something that was reported on the TV news almost every day, the worst organized crime in Japan today? Training for that? No, they hadn't done anything that seemed like training for fraud. So, what did this mean? As confusion continued to spread among the five, Ushijima continued.

"Hey, Gōriki Yasuhiro!"

Flustered at having his name suddenly called out, Gōriki was one of those who was late on the first day and had his face slapped viciously by Koshiba. Ushijima opened a file that lay in front of him and began to read from it mechanically.

"Gōriki Yasuhiro. Born December 12, 1992. Dropped out of S Technical High School. And you spent some time in a juvenile correction home for inflicting bodily injury. After getting out, you worked as an apprentice in your cousin Gōriki Masahiro's interior decorating company but after a year you got into a fight with your cousin and got reported to the police, so you quit. After that, you were a part-timer at a pub and a convenience store. You've got a sister two years younger than you who lives with your mother in the M apartments in the KT District, H City, T Prefecture. Actually, I know something about that area."

As Ushijima read this out smoothly, the face of the young man named Gōriki became paler and paler. The other four also went pale.

The basic profile was written in the CV presented at the interview, but they had no memory of mentioning any other personal information, even in idle conversation. Did they really investigate us like that? Standing in front of the five who were becoming even more agitated, Koshiba spoke as if giving the final blow.

"We've searched out the information about all of you, not just Gōriki. I'll say it again. After this you are going to be assigned to a remittance scam cell. We're going to have you work as players who call the targets. However, as we've been saying since the first day of training, we're not going to force you. Whether you do it or not is up to you. In short, it's OK if you want to quit the training at this stage, and from now we'll have nothing to do with you. Absolutely no interfering or follow-up. However!!! We have investigated thoroughly your personal information in case you cause any kind of trouble for us later. Your work experience, your family, if you've got a girl, we have her address and workplace, everything."

Even without spelling everything out, the meaning was clear. It was OK if they wanted to cut out now and not become a scam player. However, after they quit, if they ever told anyone that they had undergone fraud training, they would definitely suffer retribution by violence. Moreover, that violence might be inflicted not only on themselves but on their family and girlfriends. That was the threat.

Perhaps because of tension, at that point not a single person raised his voice to say, "I'd like to quit."

"Get it? You've got to the end of today to decide whether you're in or out."

Having made their point, Koshiba and Ushijima winked at each other and then Koshiba made a short call on his cell phone.

Then, five minutes later, a man burst into the office that was gripped in a silence that made them want to flee. Opening the door as if he would kick it open, the man seemed to be in his early 30s, his round face tanned to a shiny black, his massive chest filling his obviously expensive suit. It was Dokugawa, the veteran manager of a remittance scam cell, and now the new sub-*bantō*. As if a completely different person from the time that he had had a confidential talk with the *bantō* Kato, the large eyes in his round face glittered with ambition; he entered the room with an aura of intimidation, as if he would explode if touched.

"You the guys that lasted through the training? I'm Dokugawa, the manager that runs the scam cells."

As soon as he saw the five trainees shrink back from Dokugawa, who was vigorously spraying spittle, Koshiba's angry voice rang out much more loudly than his previous jeering.

"Hey! Why are you still seated?"

These five trainees had endured the almost military style voice training and hazing every morning and evening. They immediately jumped up, almost kicking over their chairs. The veins in Dokugawa's round, sunburned face stood out and he looked so forceful that he might kill someone on the spot. However, the next words that he said made them all feel weak in the knees.

"Er… Good evening." He spoke softly, completely different from his previous loud shouting.

"G..good evening." They all responded but they looked stupefied at the change. Koshiba and Ushijima smiled wryly.

"Well, I'm not so good at this formal stuff. Please sit down, everyone. Probably you're pretty flustered, being asked suddenly if you want to join the scam or not. However. I'm not going to say anything like you've gotta join the scam group without knowing anything about it. For young men like you, to have you do this kind of work, in a sense, will determine what your life itself will be in the future. My talk will be a little long so listen carefully, think about it carefully, and make your own decision. Got it? Whether you do it or not is up to you."

Making a rattling noise, they all sat down at their desks; then Dokugawa stood in front of the whiteboard and wrote in big red letters on the whiteboard and circled them. What he wrote was, "Is a scam really a crime?"

3.10 Is a scam really a crime?

In the silent office Dokugawa's voice rang out. From the office windows could be heard the sound of cars traveling on the highway. Outside the windows was common sense, inside the office was the absurdity of the last stage of fraud training. The participants were enveloped in a bizarre absurdity.

"First, I want everyone to think about this. Is a scam really a crime? That big guy there. What do you think?"

The man at whom he pointed was probably in his late 20s, maybe more than 180 cm tall, but he answered wearing a slightly frightened expression.

"Well… I think it's a crime, after all." Knowing that this was training for fraud, it took a lot of courage for the big guy to say it was a crime. However, Dokugawa's manner was calm, quiet, and gentle.

"Good, nice work. That's the correct answer."

The big guy seemed to breathe a small sigh of relief. However, hearing the perfectly obvious "a scam is a crime," they wondered just what this man called Dokugawa wanted to say.

"All right, let's think about it a little more deeply. What is a crime, actually?"

Each in his own way, the participants thought about crimes. Murder, robbery, rape, bodily injury, theft, fraud… After giving them sufficient time to think, Dokugawa continued.

"It's simple. A crime, first of all, is killing or injuring someone. Taking money or goods. Cheating. Finally, disturbing the order of the world. Human beings live together, right? You might think that you could live by yourself but that's a mistake. There was somebody who made the road so you could get here today. You couldn't come naked, so there was someone who made the clothes. Somebody made the train, somebody drove it, somebody supplied the power. People come together and each one does the work allotted to him, and that's what makes a society. In that society, if the crimes we were talking about earlier go unchecked, the society wouldn't be able to function, right? Essentially, there is an understanding that what we call a 'crime' is something that should not be done, so as to properly maintain this gathering of people we call society."

Slowly, as if he were teaching, Dokugawa continued to talk. For the five men gathered here, it was probably the first time for them to think about such things.

"So that's it. Now try to think a little further. When we say 'fraud,' we mean deceiving someone and taking their money. Naturally, that's a crime. But now I want you to go one step more and think carefully. Haven't you been deceived by someone, or had money, or property, or your time, or anything taken by someone? Hasn't that happened to someone you know? And isn't what happened that the one who took that from you was never arrested for fraud? What about it?"

Again, there was a moment's silence. It seemed that each of them was pulling up his own memories and experiences. Quietly, in a low but still powerful voice, Dokugawa continued.

"What about it? In the world today there are countless businesses that deceive people and take their money but are perfectly legal, aren't there? For example, what about jewelry sales? There are crooks who trick a person who has zero assets into taking out a two-million-yen loan. Or you can see on TV, those fishy health foods that nobody knows if they work or not are being sold for fabulous prices. I know that you are young, but you've been around. Even so, what about the guy who is selling teaching materials or running a school and tells you young guys who have been around that you'll definitely find work if you just get these qualifications? You pay a lot of money and get the certificate, but will you really be able to find a job? Will the work you find pay you enough for three squares a day? The guy takes your money and sells you a qualification that isn't worth a fart, and then when you find that it doesn't lead to a job, he shrugs you off by saying 'That's up to you.'"

From where he was sitting Kurusu could see all five trainees. Noticing that a few of them were nodding their heads slightly in agreement, he couldn't move a muscle. This talk was impressing them! Of course, Dokugawa too noticed this response.

"OK, now tell me this. To deceive someone and take their money is fraud. If so, why aren't the businesses I just mentioned crimes? Why aren't they arrested? Can you think why? Aren't there people everywhere who have been deceived by these kinds of sales and are stuck with loans they can't repay? Hey, Mori, what do you think about this?"

The man named Mori, suddenly called by name, was startled for an instant. Among those assembled there he seemed to be particularly young and fragile. He was probably in his early 20s and during training always looked frightened at Koshiba and Ushijima's abuse. But Mori's reply was surprisingly apt.

"Well, I guess that's because there's an actual product involved so the person who bought it did that on his own responsibility."

Hearing this, Dokugawa gave a big nod of approval. "Exactly! Even if it was a product almost like trash, since an actual product was involved, 'he had responsibility,' that is, the buyer indicated his agreement at the time of the sale, so this is not a crime. But is that really so? Actually, previously, I was a salesman for a realtor. We used to have people take out a 100% mortgage with nothing down, and these were guys who could absolutely never be able to repay a mortgage, or guys whose wife or husband suddenly fell sick and so they took out an instant loan that they couldn't repay. The banks were happy to work with us because that was the trend then. I couldn't guess how many of them had to declare personal bankruptcy because they couldn't repay. I couldn't guess how many couples, how many kids, were turned out into the streets. But if you went to look at a house that you had sold and saw that the nameplate on the door had changed, or that the house had gone to ruin, it made you feel sick to your stomach. I felt guilty. That's because I'm a softy. You can't say that the ones who are deceived are bad."

Everyone was listening attentively to this strange speech, including Kurusu, who was supposed to be a plant. It was hard to believe that these words were coming from Dokugawa, a cell manager who brought together pro scam artists who deceived people and took their money. Taking in the situation, Dokugawa again turned to the whiteboard and wrote in big letters:

1) Deceive a person who has no savings by selling him something worthless for two million yen and having him take out a loan for the full amount.

2) Deceive a person who has 20 million yen in savings and take two million yen.

Then he slapped his fist on these words and continued.

"I've been a fraudster for years, but compared to the work I did before, I've hardly had any feelings of guilt. The reason is that although this may be a crime, it's not the worst crime. Get it? Now, the amount that we take from one person is about two million yen. To you, that's a huge amount, right? If you lost that much, you'd probably hang yourself. It'd be a matter of life or death. But the ones we're taking two million yen from by a scam are the ones who have so much that they can get their hands on two million yen and cough it up the same day. Of course, they're probably sorry to lose two million yen but it's not the end of the world for them. It's not a matter of life and death to them. The reason I don't feel guilty about running these scams is that we target people who won't be hurt by losing two million yen. Even if it's ten or twenty million yen, if I take it from somebody who won't suffer very much losing even that kind of money, I don't feel guilty at all. In today's training, all of you saw the golf course and the industrial park, right? Remember what you saw. You saw luxury cars lined up at the golf course in the middle of a weekday; who do you think owns them? Those are just the kind of people we target for our scams."

3.11 A land of rich elderly people and poor young people

Memories of the parking lot at the high-class, members-only golf club that they had just seen today came back vividly to the minds of the participants. How much would it come to if you added up the cost of all of the cars parked there? One or two hundred million yen wouldn't be enough. Was there actually that much wealth in that golf course built in those hills?

Kurusu, who had also been listening attentively, was startled. The golf course story had come up, so he had to play his role as a plant because he had been instructed to do so previously. He raised his hand and was given permission to speak.

"Uh, isn't that a little off base? I understand that the members of that golf club are elderly. Even so, isn't those old geezers' money the cash that they have saved up by working hard? Isn't that the money that they need for their old age? To say you've got no feelings of guilt seems to be going a little too far. And there are also poor elderly folk too, aren't there?"

If you knew that he was a plant, this would sound farcical, but the five trainees were paying careful attention to how Dokugawa would respond to what Kurusu had said. It was working just as planned. Probably the participants too had been thinking the same thoughts.

"That may be so. Certainly, some old folks are living in poverty. And the money I'm talking about that some of them have saved up is probably the result of their having worked hard. However, numbers don't lie. We've got this data. The average amount of savings held by elderly people is twenty million yen. This doesn't even include assets like real estate; also, 60% of the total savings of all households in Japan is held by people over 60. On top of that, they're getting an average of 180,000 yen a month in pensions. That's about the same as the average monthly pay of those men you saw today working at that industrial park, but they get that money without working. Forty percent of old people who get pensions can't even spend it all and just add to their savings. So, when they die, the amount that they weren't able to use, including real estate and everything, comes to an average of thirty million yen."

Dokugawa wrote these figures precisely one by one on the whiteboard. Japan is a country of rich old people and poor young people. That concept seeped into these five men.

"To me, this just doesn't make sense. Why don't those fellows use that money that's left over? I can understand the guys who buy expensive cars and play golf. By spending their money, they give work to young people. If they buy something, the money circulates to the young people who made those things. But most old folk just stash away their money for themselves and don't use it. They just hold onto their money, glaring fiercely so that it won't be taken or it won't decrease. All over Japan, these folks who have money won't spend it, so more and more, young people, however hard they work, will never escape from poverty. The guys you saw today working at the industrial park will never get what they deserve however hard they work. They'll never be able to buy a golf club membership however many years they work. Whose fault is that? You guys, who had no money or job, answered our help wanted ad and stuck through this incredibly hard training, should know the answer better than anyone else. Am I right?"

Finally, this training was coming to an end. Dokugawa erased everything that he had written on the whiteboard and then wrote in letters larger than those he had written before, *"The elderly are Japan's cancer!"*

"The old folks in Japan are the richest in the world, and also the stingiest. While young people are crying that they have nothing to eat, I don't feel at all guilty for taking a sum like two million yen from those with money who are acting high and mighty. In fact, I feel pride in this work."

On the first day of training, if they had been talked to in this way, probably no one would have been able to agree with it in a deep sense. They probably would have thought that he was really an evil person. But now these words were deeply inscribed in the trainees' hearts.

Only five were left from the more than 20 original candidates. However they looked at it, this company was too black; they must have strongly felt like killing Koshiba and Ushijima, who ignored their human rights and treated them unthinkably, but even so they endured. They endured because they had to live. Those remaining members were desperate for money, even putting up with that torture and humiliation to earn 100,000 yen in one week, to get 300,000 yen for the month. They had their reasons for hanging on so desperately. Just to those participants, Dokugawa words were like a paradigm shift, moving them deeply.

Given that, Dokugawa did not need to say much more. He put on a final spurt.

"Sorry that I talked so much. Let me tell you what's next. Those of you who decide today, right here, to work for us, will start actual scam training from the beginning of next month. As expense money until then, we'll pay you today the 200,000 yen as we promised. Any of you who don't have a place to live, just speak up and we'll find one for you. After you actually start working at a cell, I guarantee you'll earn a minimum of 500,000 yen per month. That's what we tentatively call a transportation allowance, because we pay you 20,000 yen every day. If a scam actually is successful, your reward is a 10% commission. If the scam takes in two million yen, you get 200,000. Some guys take in fifty million yen a year, and there are legendary players who take in a hundred million. Finally, the most important thing is the fact that I, who have been in this business for years, am here today talking to you."

At this point Dokugawa stopped talking. Dokugawa, who had dirtied his hands in the fraud business for many years, was here. What did that mean? Those were the words intended to sweep away the final uneasiness that the five men assembled here still held.

"It's simple. I've never been arrested. Fraud is a business and the players who work in the cells are hardly ever caught. In fact, in the cells that I've been involved with, not a single person has been arrested. The guys who get picked up are the collectors, who work separately from the cells. You sometimes see news about a cell player being arrested but you can suppose that they just weren't on the ball. In my cell I've got very thorough protections set up so that there's no chance my players will be arrested. That's my responsibility as a cell manager. So just depend on me. I'll protect the players with my life. You guys have survived the tough selection process of a top-class scam cell. Be proud of that. Koshiba and Ushijima here really gave it to you, didn't they? You really got pounded on the head with a straw sandal, didn't you?"

The five men began to chuckle slightly at the grinning Koshiba and Ushijima.

"OK, this is the final step, when you yourselves have to make the decision. I've said everything I wanted to say. Fraud is not the worst crime. You'll make piles of money and never get pinched. If you stick with us, your worries about how you will live, your empty hopes, your frustrations, are all gone. The choice is yours. That's all."

The intelligent-looking man named Mori bit his lips as if he had made up his mind. The eyes of the punk named Gōriki were sparkling. The big guy seemed to be moved by what Dokugawa had said and almost had tears in his eyes.

"All of them are going to stay with us." Dokugawa, Koshiba, Ushijima, and also Kurusu felt this strongly and in fact that was the way it turned out. On that day, the five trainees all made the decision to work as scam players.

As the finale, Koshiba shouted in his gravelly voice that seemed to stick to their ears, "OK, everybody, on your feet!"

With a whooshing sound they all stood up and stood straight and perfectly still.

"Now, for the last thing, our usual speaking exercise! Good morning!"

Interrupting the five men who were about to repeat automatically, Dokugawa gave Koshiba a hard knock on the head. "Wait, wait, wait! Koshiba, if you start shouting at this late hour, you'll bother the neighbors!"At this some of the trainees began to laugh freely. Having endured the harsh training, they had been chosen. If they stuck to this work, they would make money so that their lives would be completely changed from what they were. That gave them hope. A strong bond was born among these five who had endured.

3.12 The justification[17] for preying on the elderly

The motivation for becoming a scam cell player is extraordinarily high. The more I continued my interviews, the more keenly I felt this. None of them spare effort or study; they learn, they contrive, and make efforts to take the most money from the elderly in the most efficient way. How is this motivation cultivated? It would be a long story to understand in detail the inner workings of their minds, but I combined in this example the details of the training given by several fraud organizations gleaned from my interviews.

In a manner of speaking, this is brainwashing. In fact, both the members who have experience in underworld

[17] *Taigi meibun*, here translated as "justification," originally meant "the right relations between the emperor and his subjects" or "supreme duty of righteousness and correspondence of name and status." Brownlee, J. S. (1997). *Japanese historians and the national myths, 1600-1945*, UBC Press, pp. 33, 121, 125, 228n8).

businesses, who are the seed players among the scam player candidates, and the novice players who are new recruits like the five remaining men here, must undergo training as new scam players before they are assigned to a cell, and here more explicit brainwashing techniques are used.

The person who served as the model for Koshiba, a coach of the training session described above, agreed to be interviewed and made this statement. He said that the brainwashing method for fraud training is done along the lines of so-called self-help seminars.

"The first important point is residential training. It's often said that residential training is done to isolate them in an environment from which they can't escape, but in scam training, it's a little different; creating a team spirit is the most important thing. Sometimes we rent a mountain retreat, sometimes we room at an office in the sticks. When we stay at an office, they go to a nearby sauna or someplace to take a bath, so it's not at all an environment from which they can't escape."

In fact, the training for scam cell operations does not take much time. The training for the new players who have experience in underworld businesses is, as noted above, to send them to other cells that are in operation and have them memorize the script. After they memorize it, they watch actual performances by experienced players and the coach, and do role playing (joining a three-man team and taking turns playing the victim and other roles); with that, the training for scam operations is finished.

However, the man I interviewed who was the model for Koshiba insisted that the brainwashing training that is added to this practical training is the most important point of fraud training.

"What we do is 'negative training' and 'positive training.' For example, the '50 failures.' What this is, we have the candidates sit in a circle and have each one of them tell about the mistakes they have made in their lives. Then for each one all the others say what they think about it, but we've made two rules: Absolutely do not show pity, and do not make excuses. We take our time and pursue thoroughly whether the cause of all those mistakes was in themselves. This is your typical negative training, but the point is to make the speaker himself realize that all his mistakes were his own fault. Not somebody else's fault, not the fault of situation he's in, but it's his own fault because he himself, at each point, did not make the best choice or enough effort."

This negative training is so severe that it has been given such daunting names as "ganging up" or "thorough thrashing." When they have finished presenting their fifty mistakes, most people's personality is in a state of collapse.

"If some guy starts to go berserk, we hold him down by brute force. In that situation some of them give up calling themselves human beings, and some guys even piss their pants. Everyone has to take one turn. The important thing is to do this in the middle of the night. After that, as far as negative training goes, we do it only at the first session, even as part of fraud training. Because it's dangerous."

Then, the player candidates, who have been completely deprived of their self-esteem by this negative training, are now given the complete opposite: positive training. It begins with applause.

"First, you've got to praise them a lot for having lasted through the negative training. The typical person couldn't bear up under that hell. You tell them that it's a great thing to take a square look at the mistakes in your life, but you guys who have done that thoroughly should now be able to make the necessary choices and efforts when the time comes for the rest of your life. Your life up to now was not so good because you always put the blame for your mistakes somewhere else, but it'll be different from now! You keep praising them to the skies!"

Positive training begins with praise, but it has several patterns, for example, the "30-million-yen dream."

"For the kind of guy who is a scam player, 30 million yen is the goal. We run a presentation session where they have to say how they would use that kind of money.

When we make everyone tell their dream, the other guys in the group will get all excited and yell, 'That's small potatoes! You could do a lot more!' Sometimes we have a guy who's actually succeeded at scams tell them what his life has been like afterwards, and sometimes at this point we show them the actual cash. We make it seem real to them by telling them that they too can earn this kind of money. We do this kind of positive training at the end-of-the-day assembly when they're working at a cell, or during the waiting period when a cell has closed and they're waiting for their next project. We've also had a veteran who's earned a lot of money come around in the most expensive car he owns and give them a talk."

At the close of the positive training, everyone forms a circle and gives three cheers: "We can do it! Can do it! Can do it!"

"I've heard that at some other cells they even have them go jogging in the morning, shouting, 'One two three four, it's meeee!' Of course, at the 'it's me' at the end, they burst out laughing."

There are examples of many other kinds of training but what they have in common are the following justifications that are imbued into the minds of the trainees:

- Fraud is admirable work.
- Players who are admitted to a cell are chosen people just by the fact of being admitted.
- Fraud is a crime, but it is not the worst crime. That is because it is a business method that takes an amount of money from people who can afford to pay that amount, so the degree of harm the victims suffer is small, and there are many unsavory businesses that are legal.
- It is a crime to take money from the elderly by scams but there is justice in that. The elderly who hold onto their money without spending it are the enemies of the younger generations and the cancer of Japan.
- By earning all you can here, your life from now on will certainly change.

This cannot be called anything but brainwashing, but to

the cell players these justifications were exceedingly apt and deepened their brainwashing even further. The reason is perfectly obvious.

That is, the only problem in these justifications is the statement that fraud is a crime; all the other statements are perfectly legitimate. That Japan's seniors hoard their wealth and do not stimulate the economy by spending it, that young people are earning less and less and are concerned about their future, that unscrupulous business methods of players who are never arrested are rampant, all of these are perfectly true. Therefore, this imprinting very strongly activates the economic resentment of young people, whose economic compensation is extremely little however much they exert themselves. In addition, there are men that attract these young players strongly, namely, the cell supervisors: *bantō* such as Kato, who appeared earlier in this narrative, and cell managers such as Dokugawa.

3.13 The aura emanating from the status of **bantō**

In a certain month of a certain year, in the coffee shop in the third-floor lobby of a certain downtown hotel in Tokyo, I saw a 33-year-old man sprawled comfortably on a sofa, and I thought, "That's the type." He was wearing pointed wingtip shoes and colored chinos in a sedate shade; he sat with his hips implanted deeply into the sofa and his legs spread slightly apart. Above, he wore a matching polo shirt but the sleeve openings were bulging with his thick arms, something like a pro athlete. His face was lightly tanned, and he wore a hunting cap embroidered with a small tribal pattern; these gave rise to sense of volatile delinquency.

"I rose to become a *bantō* two years ago. I moved up from being a cell player. The qualifications for being a *bantō*? Well, let's see. It's a pretty dull story but first, I suppose, is the number of years you've been working, like a company employee. The number of years you've continued to work as a player without ever betraying the ones above you is important. Because from the backers' point of view, for someone whom they've put money into to drop out or something, that's out of the question, you see."

His attitude was bold as he looked directly into my eyes. What I could feel from his bright, healthy expression was manliness and shrewdness. His gestures, brimming with energy and self-confidence, made him seem almost as if he was acting.

This was the *bantō* status. In the investigations I have done up to now, I have met only a few *bantō*, but in every case I cannot forget the strong impression I got when I met them for the first time. Kawada, this 33-year-old *bantō*, was also a man who gave off something like a threatening aura. I'm not sure how to express it but it was an atmosphere that made one feel intuitively that this was a man you could trust, and entrust yourself to him. He had a fine voice. He was expressive, collected, personable, and forceful.

I asked several persons connected to fraud what the conditions for being promoted to *bantō* were, and I list them here.

- The ability to talk tough (the ability to manage a cell by the voice of authority).
- Very curious but very cautious.
- Not squeezed by debt.
- Absolutely no drug use.
- Not much of a gambler. Someone who likes gambling is not qualified to be promoted to *bantō*.
- Moderate in his own pleasures but is willing to spend money on others (likes to treat).
- Cannot be pugnacious. What position will he take in the event of trouble, which will certainly arise in the organization?
- Has wide personal connections and the ability to gather people.
- Is able to train players.

It is clear that, within the criminal business of fraud, these are just the characteristics necessary for drawing people together and managing them as a stable group. However, my impression from my interviews is that in the end the *bantō* were not chosen just on the basis of their personality or their manliness. Kawada, too was typical. He was a man who thought deeply about the feelings of the cell players who worked under him.

"In a sense I can't deny that what I do is a black business. Talking about black, the guys who drop out just complain, but don't the ones who remain have high motivation? After all, even in Chinese noodle shops or pubs, there's a feeling of unity among the staff—they strive to develop themselves and like, even with low pay, everyone pulls together and supports the shop. The scam cell is a black business with plenty of what you might call social insurance and good pay. It's true enough we use the thinking of a black business as a means to pick out the ones you can use at a cell. But the social insurance at a scam cell is a lot better than at any other business."

In fact, at the cells that Kawada manages, extensive social insurance is provided in addition to the incentive of the take from the scam profits that are paid to the players.

For example, the cost of any additional training that the players get is borne by the *bantō*. There are also many cells in which this cost is borne by the players themselves. He even has established a reserve fund in case someone is arrested. Even if one or two from the cell are arrested, if they stand up to police questioning and don't give up the higher-ups, their job and livelihood after they are released from prison are guaranteed. There is even a family allowance paid to players who have a wife and children.

Horizontal relationships among the players themselves are limited; however, on occasions such as the closing of a cell or a "great fever" (when a large amount of money is taken from one victim), celebratory parties are held where they go on a spree. *Bantō* also hold parties to send off a player who is retiring after earning a great deal of money. They offer consultations when a former player starts a business with the money he has earned, or consultations concerning personal connections. They even give advice about personal matters.

"A *bantō* has to earn a lot just to be able to do all that, but the guys in the cells are always saying that the money they earn is not for themselves but should be used for others. If you just store it up and take profits only for yourself, there is the possibility of being 'knocked' (having the money taken in scams stolen). When you're involved in a shady business, people come to hate you or be jealous of you, and you get stabbed in the back. On the other hand, when juvenile delinquents try to run a business, they'll use up all the assets and just loaf around. If you spend lavishly you'll attract the attention of the police, but basically, they say that you should use the money for your own generation and your juniors. Whether we go drinking at a cabaret or make the rounds of the dives, or hold some kind of event, it's always in our minds that we're treating our subordinates with the money that we got from scams."

Take money from the elderly, the "cancer of Japan" who save up their money without spending it and return that money to the next generation. Because the means of doing that is fraud, there are limits to how much it can be legitimized, but in my investigations, I met even those who would go so far as to tell jokes or put on airs. After the Great East Japan Earthquake of 2011, there were *bantō* who contributed an enormous amount for the youth and children of the afflicted areas. It was an amount comparable to several years' salary for the typical company employee. Immediately afterward, the same persons were working out scam scenarios targeting the elderly living in the afflicted areas, showing that their "typical evenhandedness" and "sense of justice" was operating in this case too. At the least, one strong feeling is born here in the cell players working under them. It is adoration of the *bantō* and cell manager.

3.14 The successful person right before young people's eyes

It is very easy to understand. For the cell players, the *bantō* and the cell manager are "images of successful people" right before their eyes. What made me keenly aware of this overwhelming unifying force in fact was not fraud; when I was investigating the actual conditions in the field of construction and public works, where the workforce is getting older and the number of young candidates is declining rapidly, this was a phrase that I heard from the bosses in that business.

"You talk to other bosses, it's the same story in the end. After all, bosses like us aren't cool so the youngsters don't want to come in. When we were kids, our families were poor and we hated study, so we would round up some juvie kids from junior high and made motorcycle gangs. Then when we quit that, we were picked up by the local gangsters doing construction and public works, and given a job. The bosses and the older workmen tooled around in big cars with a girl with big tits sitting in the passenger seat, and treated us to drinks to our fill, so wouldn't you call that cool? So we thought that if we became workmen we'd become grownups like that. But the guys that we were then are now the bosses, but we're not earning that much money. My car is a minivan. The wife is in the passenger seat and the kids are in the back. Just the bosses get together with their families for a weekend barbecue, and the young guys are thinking, 'What the hell is that?'"

This speech was persuasive. It is a fact that young people today are starved for images of successful people near them. They have no goal that says, "if I take this job, I'll become that kind of person." On the other hand, there is a tendency for this young generation to become the so-called "mild *yankī*" or "soft *yankī*."[18] The inclination to move to Tokyo, or to better themselves, is weak; they hang out with their local friends of the same generation; they don't have any big dreams and just help each other out on their low wages. Given this mentality, they are satisfied to some extent. This is the image of young people today.

However, even in this group, there are young people

[18] See page 4, note 6.

with a strong desire to better themselves. Within the mild *yankī* strata, the ones with an exceptionally strong desire to succeed tend to be treated as the "try hard guys" but that is because the mild *yankī* as a group are resigned to their fate, having no image of a successful person nearby. What happens to the young men with such a strong desire to better themselves that they stand out in that group, when they see a *bantō* like Kawada? What they feel is admiration for the *bantō* and others who are successful people. Then comes an acute sense of being a member of the elite: "Only we know the route to success! "Only we know really cool seniors!"

Among young players are some who say things like this: "I could never tell my hometown friends that I'm running scams because they would treat me as an outcast or a fool. They'd think it's something to be ashamed of. But I think that they're the ones who are fools. We earn in a month what they take in in a year. It's a different world. They've just been broken down by poverty and have no aspirations."

Even among the strata of young so-called delinquents, there is the feeling that earning a living by fraud is uncool. They say, "When you have plenty of money, people stop coming close to you." Statements like that are a little difficult for someone born in the Shōwa period (1926-1989) to understand. In today's Japan, there is the sense that a young person with money is probably doing something suspicious.

However, the frostier the surroundings become, the more the players who have a strong desire to better themselves take fire. In other words, they are mild *yankī* whose way of thinking has been changed, or people who are too fired up ever to become a mild *yankī*. Further, the overly "black" training system for nurturing scam players succeeds in skillfully extracting this kind of human resource from a pool of impoverished and sluggish young men.

The above is the reason why preying on the elderly has expanded to this extent. It is an undeniable fact that in Japan, wealth is concentrated in the elderly while young people are starving. In this contemporary Japan, they are brainwashed into justifying preying on the elderly, or rather they believe it implicitly. Further, they have self-esteem from having survived a selection process even more severe than that of a black business. They admire the men in the higher ranks, who provide an image of successful men close to them, men who possess overwhelmingly the power to draw people together and the "aesthetics of redistribution"; they feel strongly a strong sense of elitism by belonging to such a group.

This is in fact why preying on the elderly can never end. These motivated young players will not hesitate to deceive older people and take their money, even if their business is not fraud. The reason I wrote at the beginning of Chapter 2, that knowing their methods is meaningless, is here; after all, considering their mentality, if they are able to take money from the elderly, the means don't matter.

Further, as long as they have this mentality and sense of elitism, they would never consider giving up those in the higher ranks, who are their benefactors, so even in the unlikely event that a cell is exposed, it is extremely unlikely that the police investigation would reach the higher ranks. If a cell is destroyed as a result of exposure, the top ranks would remain and, as explained in the previous chapter, all they have to do is once again nurture players with a strong consciousness.

Actually, high in the clouds where the players cannot see them, are the bloodsucking backers. They are the bloodsuckers who have young people prey on the elderly though their investments, while remaining in a safe place and not dirtying their hands.

However, even if the cell players know about them, they would still not sell out the top ranks to the police because the backers provide capital and maintain the fraud infrastructure so young people can eat. The fundamental belief of the cell players is that, compared to the elderly, who just store up their money and begrudge spending it even for themselves, even the bloodsucking backers are more righteous.

Chapter 4

What kind of people prey on the elderly? The real image as seen in four actual examples

4.1 Players' backgrounds changed drastically

What sort of young people make the rounds of the cells as players employed in scams preying on the elderly? What are the backgrounds of the youth who engage in criminal fraud with such high motivation? First, I will provide a rough overview.

Around 2003, when "It's me!" scams began to increase rapidly, people from the loan-sharking business and persons owing multiple debts formed the kernel of the scam cells. Loan sharks, who then were charging exorbitant interest rates and using violent collection methods such as demanding repayment by telling debtors to sell their internal organs, were facing a period of significant change with the imminent revision to the law (act for countermeasures against usury, passed in the 156th ordinary Diet session in 2003); the leading members of the illegal loan businesses affiliated with the Goryōkai gangster group, which was said to be the most influential in loan sharking, were arrested, and their cells were disbanded. In such a situation, it was only natural that among those who had been managers or staff workers in the usury business, some would leave that business and develop the next ones. Among those new businesses was the "It's me!" scam.

Thus, it was just because the scam players of the early stage were those with experience in loan sharking that the backer-*bantō*-affiliated cell hierarchy of the scam associations was an exact copy of the Goryōkai loan sharking organization; moreover, they developed an evolved version by isolating each layer to protect the upper ranks from arrest.

People carrying multiple loans were included among the players in the early days because they were being made to work in the scam cells to pay off their loans; many of these people also were made to work as bagmen (at that time, "withdrawers"), being used as expendable staff who could be arrested.

However, the attributes of the players changed rapidly with the passage of time. First, the ones who entered the trade to assist the former loan sharks in conducting successful scams more efficiently were those who were engaged as young players in underground businesses from the 1990s into the 21st century. They were the elite of the so-called unscrupulous sales personnel, involved in everything from crooked door-to-door sales, sales methods using hypnosis, romance scams, and sales of training courses for qualifications,[19] all the way to pyramid sales schemes. They were valuable human resources that sustained the fraud business: some of them became players themselves; others worked in the background as trainers of players, scenario writers, or developers of contacts with name list dealers.

The next people to enter the business were juvenile delinquents from Tokyo and its environs. Scam cells with players in their teens and managers around 20 years old began to appear but they were what is called "participants by connections." I frequently heard that the people who became players at that time got started when their seniors, local delinquents who originally had worked in loan sharking and had now changed their trade to fraud, used their contacts to scout and train them.

The thoroughly rationalized organization, as described in chapters one and two, that originally was centered on people from underground businesses and juvenile delin-

---

[19] "Training courses for qualifications" are sets of materials for self-study or by correspondence to prepare for license examinations in a wide variety of fields, from cultural skills such as calligraphy or foreign languages to professions such as tour guiding, dental technician, or TV repair.

quents, was completely established by the end of 2005.

For a while after that time there was no big change in the attributes of the personnel, but from around 2008 a new type began to be seen in larger numbers; these were people from the wider society such as men with experience working in typical enterprises and graduates fresh from universities.

There were two reasons for this. First was the arrival of the severe recession brought about by the Lehman Shock.[20] Those who were destitute, such as laid-off contract workers, dismissed employees, and Internet café refugees,[21] were actively enrolled in the collection corps. It was a very rare case but one person I interviewed had risen from that level to become a player.

The second reason is that in addition to the fraud scenarios that had been typical up to that time, such as impersonating a family member ("It's me!"), billing fraud, and advance-fee loan scams, financial types of remittance scams such as fraud involving unlisted shares or corporate debentures made their appearance. The "It's me!" scam, which is known as a "one-shot type" in the field, in fact involves a theatrical phone call to take the money that same day in a one-shot deal. In contrast, the financial types of remittance scams require producing printed materials and Internet sites to promote the fake investment, and in some cases actually registering a corporation (of course, a paper company) and setting up a bank account, so these require cells that can operate for a comparatively longer time and players that have a high level of training.

People with business experience and college graduates possessed the background knowledge required for such kinds of frauds; I have heard of cases in which persons who had actually worked previously in brokerage firms dropped out and joined a cell, and cases in which a person was caught in a honey trap, semi-forced to join a fraud organization, and made into the brain of the outfit.

[20] Refers to the collapse of the Lehman Brothers investment bank in 2008.

[21] People living in Internet cafes because they cannot afford regular housing.

These were the basic changes in the human resources that made up the scam cells. However, the key point here is that for most of these people the "justification" described in the last chapter suited them admirably. I would like to analyze closely the mentality of those who have devoted themselves to the work of fraud from a few cases from my interviews.

4.2 Case 1: A player in loan-sharking-type advance-fee loan fraud changes his profession

Kanbe Hashiru. He was born in Tokyo in 1980. He grew up in an apartment complex in Tokyo with his mother, who was a nurse, and a younger brother. His uncles and his grandfather were alcoholics who loved to gamble, and repeatedly borrowed money using his mother's name so from his youth he lived in a harsh environment where debt collectors were always barging into his home and the freshly severed head of a cat was once hung on the washing machine next to the entrance. From elementary school age he turned to crimes such as theft and extortion, and was sent to a reformatory for robbery resulting in bodily injury. Even so, after his release he continued his trade in violent robberies with two friends that he had met in the reformatory. However, while robbing the proceeds of an escort club, they met with a counterattack, were abducted, and were beaten with an iron bar to within an inch of their lives.

At that time, the uncle of one of his friends, a currently active yakuza boss, mediated for them, and through his introduction, Kanbe began working in the loan sharking business, but a dark period lasted for some time after that. He worked at the lowest job, collecting money from debtors, but he was too softhearted and showed sympathy to the debtors, so his results were poor, and he was demoted to a cell for advance-fee loan scams (a fraud in which money is loaned but a security fee is taken before the loan contract is signed). He achieved a modest success in this fraud, but in the end financial area work just did not suit him and he continued to be in the dumps. Afterwards, together with friends from the reformatory (one was the manager of a loan sharking shop, and the other was a member of a group of young yakuza), he requested an introduction and joined an "It's me" scam cell as a player. There he became a "four-point" player (one who had achieved an annual income of 40 million yen), and in just three years he rose to the position of *bantō*, and further advanced to the status of backer.

Concerning Kanbe's background and how he rose to become a *bantō* and then to the top as a backer, my book *Furikomi hanzai kessha* [*Remittance Fraud Organizations*] (Takarajimasha, 2013) describes his and his friends' younger days. However, he is an unusual type even among the typical scam players that originally were loan sharks.

"Most of those who went from moneylending to running scams are of two types: either the guys at the top who wanted to make use of the money they had made in loan sharking, or the ones who went into scams because they couldn't make any money from loans. There are lot of guys who think that 'making money is the be all and end all,' whatever the means, and in fact most of them were brought up in poverty. It's paying back the bastards that made fun of them when they were kids, or bragging that they were earning ten times the amount of those the same age who took the usual course of high school and college; for them, the moneylending business was a kind of revenge. You also see a lot of guys who are like hosts,[22] and so on.

"On that point, in my case anyway, all I can say is that moneylending just didn't suit me. Really, when I was in the money-lending game, I was just good for nothing, When I pushed for repayments and someone started crying on me, I just couldn't get tough with them. I grew up seeing my mom in tears and kneeling on the ground in front of the loan sharks, so I just couldn't get that memory out of my mind. The vicious moneylenders are

---

[22] "Hosts" are the male counterpart of the hostesses in Japanese bars and clubs; their work is to entertain female customers by serving them drinks, engaging them in conversation, etc.

the lowest of the low, so I had to switch to advance-fee loan scams. Here I made some money, but I was rotting. In the end, isn't the business of taking money from people who don't have any money as low as it gets? So when a guy like me can bring off one ["It's me" scam], we feel oddly refreshed. It's because I have been freed from bullying weak people, but also, I have the feeling that I've finally found respectable work."

As I wrote above, at first, it was a veteran of the loan sharking business that drew him into remittance frauds, but at that time the candidates for that business were often former juvenile delinquents: their parents were destitute; they were abused in body and mind or abandoned as infants; they were drug addicts; their parents were completely depraved from the start; or they were taken from such parents and grew up in an orphanage; etc.

Youths who are not blessed with a good home environment turn to delinquency and band together with friends who share the same troubles to form gangs, which are then enrolled by local motorcycle gangs and so on, and in the end become absorbed by the local yakuza, or find urban-type work such as on-site staff for construction and public works, or in the sex industry. The stereotypical image of the Shōwa-type[23] delinquent was a picture that still existed unchanged even in Japan of the 1990s. One outlet for them that became conspicuous in the late 1990s was the loan sharking business.

What kind of psychology was operating here? The generation that was working as players on the scene in the loan sharking business in the period from the late 1990s through 2003, which was the germination period of fraud, had memories of the bubble period. What arose naturally in them was economic resentment of those of the same generation who were financially well-off.

"We all have a complex. We grew up in some shitty housing project but in our generation, there were a lot of guys who were what we called 'rich juvies.' Maybe it was only in Tokyo but there were the teamers[23] who hung out in Shibuya, and there were a lot of guys who went to really fancy high schools. From our point of view, they didn't really fit in; the guys who spent big money to go to school did some mugging. If they got allowances from their parents, why didn't they stay home with their big TVs and video games; that's what we thought then because we did a little simple robbery. Guys from the Kantō Rengō[24] or someplace would come to Shibuya hunting for the teamers and the situation became really tense. It was that kind of situation when we were afraid that we too were going to get mixed up in it. Anyway, that was just a poor guy's inferiority complex; it's for sure that in the same generation as those doing loan sharking there were a lot of guys who, because of that complex, would say to themselves, 'I'll show you! By the time I'm 25 I'll be living on one of the top floors of a tower condo!' I felt that tension too. But somehow, I just couldn't get into moneylending as a business, so I started doing scams and I finally felt as if I had found the right adversary."

This Kanbe pulled in a fantastic amount after he became a scam player. After he was promoted to *bantō*, he was a ringleader who frequently conducted "player training by a *bantō*," which basically was strictly forbidden (it was seen as too risky for a *bantō* to come in contact with player candidates as long as there was a possibility that some might drop out), where he would plant in the players' minds the justification that taking small change from the elderly who are holding on to so much money is not the worst crime.

The picture we can make from Kanbe's words, who was a living dictionary from the early days of remittance scams (i.e., preying on the elderly), is that those scams embraced the destitute young people who held economic resentment against the rich of their own generation, which has existed throughout history, and caused a shift to economic resentment against the elderly in the top layer of society

---

[23] One kind of juvenile delinquent.

[24] A motorcycle gang.

who were holding onto all of the money.

4.3 Case 2: Please tell me if there is a sales position in a company that is not "black"

Yamano Ryō. He was an only child, born in 1990 in Shizuoka Prefecture. While in elementary school he was an ace striker on a local youth soccer team but when he was in junior high school his parents divorced and the household's economic situation worsened. The cause of the divorce was his mother's reverse psychological domestic violence toward his father; after losing his job, his father did not seek new employment and he was supported by his mother. She abandoned her parental rights and he lived with his father, who began work delivering newspapers, but the family's economic situation did not improve so he gave up his hopes for soccer although he had earned the slot of regular player from the third term of his first year in junior high.

Afterwards, he entered a local part-time high school but had to drop out when his father again became unemployed, and through the introduction of a local senior he worked for three years in the construction and demolition business. He further had experience as a salesman in a direct marketing firm (making sales visits cold or by telephone appointment).

This company was an ultra-sports-oriented black company that had a quota for squats every morning when he came to work. The merchandise was mainly health foods and beauty supplies; the company was the typical unscrupulous telephone sales type. Originally a genuinely athletic person, he found this company suitable to him, but through an introduction from this company's manager he began to work as a cell player in an investment type of remittance scam. In his first month he set a record by taking in 20 million yen.

Yamano was the athletic type and had participated in team sports so in a manner of speaking was a true-born scam player. He boasted that the scam cell training and so on "was a cinch." In fact, the reason that there are quite a few persons in scam cells who were active in sports when young is that the athlete's temperament is a good fit for this business. Further, a child that continues to play sports is a big economic burden on his parents so there are many cases in low-income households in which the child had to withdraw from sports unwillingly. Also, even if one spends one's youth in competitions, earning a living as a professional is not easy unless one is an outstanding athlete; another possible factor is the big gap between the brilliance of life as a pro athlete and life after one retires. (For example, in 2014, a 25-year-old former athlete who had competed in the Inter-High[25] swimming competition was arrested.)

Yamano says that he is grateful to the manager at his former company who introduced him to the world of fraud.

"You can call him a manager, but he was really a semi-gangster.[26] He went right into that sales company after junior high and got training. He knew a lot of people—junior high classmates, friends who were yakuza or semi-gangsters. A lot of sales companies are considered to be black companies, but things aren't so easy that a guy who has been knocked around and can't survive a war of attrition would be kept on in a management position. That's just wishful thinking; in the first place, sales itself is black, isn't it? If the sales department of a typical firm did that it would be a big problem, so they outsource it to a sales company, don't they? So it's only natural that sales com-

---

[25] All Japan Inter High School Athletic Meeting, an annual competition sponsored by the Japanese High School Sports Association. The suspect was Yamada Taiji.

[26] *Hangure*: loosely organized criminal gangs not considered as yakuza; non-officially designated organized-crime groups. "The investigative journalist Atsushi Mizoguchi coined a term for these outlaws: hangure. It comes from han (half), and gurentai—undisciplined youth gangs in the chaotic postwar period who preyed on the general population, engaging in theft, robbery and violent crimes. The "half" in the term is also a nod to the fact these new groups are half-yakuza, as many are backed by yakuza or ex-yakuza who can no longer operate in the open — and so have no code of honor to burden them." Adelstein, J. (2013, April 7). What's with the police purge on dance clubs? *The Japan Times*. https://www.japantimes.co.jp/news/2013/04/07/national/whats-with-the-police-purge-on-dance-clubs/#.WrBwp5cuDcs

panies are black.

"I really hate the jerks who drop out of that kind of company and, putting on like they're a victim, get on the Internet and grumble something like 'the company I joined was too black—LOL.' My generation is just trash. All they can do is complain. I prefer the old guys who are managers grumbling in some bar that 'that was the rule in companies in the old days.' Anyway, guys in a scam cell who complain are beaten, aren't they? That's refreshing, isn't it?"

Yamano was drawn to working as a scam player by the perfection of the "theory of the victor in the sales field," that it was completely clear-cut. His motivation was heightened by the facts that everyone in his cell was motivated, and no one was there who shouldn't have been there.

"To run scams, the most important thing is keeping high motivation. First, if you're going to run the business as a pro, it's important to have an attractive product. I would say that if a sales pro has self-confidence, he would want to work in a place that deals in attractive products because joining a place like that means a step up in your career. The scam target's being elderly people, marketing is the natural approach; the scam can make the product seem ever so attractive. After all, the product is a fiction. Even if it's not a case of fraud, in today's world most companies have as their goal some means of getting hold of the money that elderly people have, so as far as a sales agency is concerned, it makes no difference whether the product is real or imaginary. It's perfectly simple and pure, so you can't go wrong."

What surprised me listening to Yamano was that there were almost too many points in common between the sales company that he had worked for and his scam cell, except for whether the products they handled were real or imaginary. In a manner of speaking, was the scam cell a black company in which there were only winners? Or rather it might be better to see a scam cell as a black company that paid appropriate wages. For Yamano, being a player at a scam cell was a sacred calling.

"Of course, you have to consider that there is the risk of being arrested, but that would mean just five or eight years. This is something I heard secondhand from my *bantō*, but even if you get eight years, you'd still have a lot more money than what you could earn in eight years at a typical job in the outside world; it's that kind of thinking. At the sales company where I used to work, I earned a lot and accordingly lived in a nice place and spent freely on having a good time, so I could save only about 500,000 yen per year. If I stayed as a rank-and-file employee and that company lasted for eight years (though probably it wouldn't last that long), when I added it up, I thought it was stupid. I'd work my butt off in that sales company and I was sure I could earn more than the other guys, but in the end, it would come to just four million yen.

"Maybe you can't put a price on the time I would lose spending eight years in jail, but it would be at least ten times that, 40 million yen, that I would have before I got caught, so I think that I would be the winner. People say that the guys in a scam cell will never be arrested, but you can never tell what will happen in the future. So I'm thinking that I'll save up 40 million yen and hide it carefully, so it won't be found even if I'm arrested, and then let them arrest me after that. To put it another way, when I save up 40 million yen, I'll retire."

Yamano added that after he had saved up 40 million yen, "I'll manage a black sales company or work as a scam coach."

4.4 Case 3: Isn't university a scam?

Mori Yōsuke. He was born in 1991 and spent his childhood with his mother and two older sisters in a prefecture in the southern part of the Kanto area. He says that he didn't stand out particularly and that he was a kid who disliked standing out. One sister became a nurse and got married; the other dropped out of university and became a care worker. Mori was the only one who liked studying to some extent, took a junior high entrance test, and entered a combined junior-senior high school. However, it was not a particularly high-ranking school. His household was that of a single mother because his parents had divorced when he was an infant; his mother was employed at a hospital as a pharmacist. However, when Mori was a high school senior, she contracted a serious illness and was hospitalized for two months. Afterwards, Mori entered the communications faculty of a science university in another prefecture and began to live alone, but he was disappointed in his hope to enter the pharmacology department.

One day, while he was a student, he happened to visit his mother's apartment and saw some documents that had been put into his mother's mailbox. From them he learned that her apartment rent, management fees, and resident association dues had not been paid for a long time. Talking with his mother, he learned that she owed a large amount in consumer loans, and that after her illness she had changed jobs to work at a pharmacy where her salary was half what it had been before, and that she was now looking for a job. His mother and his sisters didn't get along and had practically broken off relations, and his grandparents had died while still young, so Mori proposed that he would drop out of university and look for work, but at his mother's strong insistence he stuck it out until graduation. However, when he started searching for a job, he got rejections from dozens of companies even though he was a science major. In his senior year, through a connection who was doing systems work part-time for an online dating site, he went to work immediately after graduation in a fictitious claim fraud, and at present is a spot player (a player who works at his convenience) at an "It's me" scam cell.

Mori was a novice who, as described in the previous chapter, underwent training and was then placed in a scam cell; his first impression was that "It was black!"

"Right in the middle of a scam cell, I was really up in the air. Like I was from another culture, the atmosphere was different, everybody there had come in under different circumstances, but after all, fraud is a crime. You hear a lot about college grads who are players in scam cells but usually they gather in their own cells; it is rare for someone like me who is a college grad to suddenly be dropped into an "It's me!" scam cell.

"Concerning the other guys, the look in their eyes was different, because for them it was normal to get a beating on the job. One thing I felt strongly when I made the jump from fictitious claims to "It's me" was that their glare was the real thing. At first, I kind of misunderstood and thought they were just stupid juvies because in fact, there were some really unbelievable guys there. For example, one guy asked me, 'What's Windows?' He was about the same age as me. You can hardly believe that he was born and brought up in Japan!"

However, Mori also was exposed to the deadly poison that was the overwhelming motivation of the scam players, which was by no means normal. After working at the cell for a few weeks, he began to look at the other players with respect.

"First, I learned what they meant when they said, 'After all, there's no scam like the "It's me!"' Of course, the amount they earned was spectacular but their concentration when they were making calls was something else. They were all extremely hard workers and they never took off work. Besides that, our cell moved its location every two weeks. In the intervals we would have some light-weight training or something like a seminar, and we would each present what we wanted to do with the money we were earning here, and what we wanted to be doing five or ten years from now. The guys working there were all specific. And there were guys who not only had specific plans but were already making preparations to carry them out. In any case, when I was in junior high, senior high, and college, I never met guys who were so focused. What was typical was to think casually about what kind of work they wanted to do and how much they wanted to make. For myself, I didn't think of anything but paying off my mother's debts. If some job came up, I'd quit what I was doing and go for that; my thinking was shallow. So I thought that those guys were really something, far beyond me."

At the "It's me!" scam cell to which Mori belonged, the questions in the dummy training described in the previous chapter, "Is fraud the worst crime? Aren't there other crimes that are worse?" were asked while the cell was in operation. Mori says that his thoughts at that time have now become his emotional pillars.

"I thought really hard and began to think that the worst fraud in Japan was school, including not only university but also high school too. Of course, I know that people who have gotten an education at university are supporting Japan, but even so, for example, originally I wanted to go to a pharmacology department but that takes six years, and if my mother paid for everything that would come to 20 million yen, including living expenses. Of course, you would make a fair income, but it would take years just to break even. Pharmacy is not too bad but a humanities department or a F-rank school (a bottom-line university) are one hundred percent frauds, aren't they? They make you pay a lot of money and sell you a dream of some kind of campus life, but then after you graduate you can't get a job to earn back what it cost. There are guys who say that 'college grads can choose their work' but that's just bull-shit. Because they had the time and money to go to col-lege, it's only natural that they wouldn't choose a job that's not worth it.

"I was just a shallow person who, until I learned about my mother's debts, never thought even once that our household was poor, but anyways what percent of Japa-nese people say there's a need to send your kids to a university and have them graduate? It's a fact that out of all the developed countries, only in Japan do the parents pay the total amount of college tuition fees, but even if they made it free of charge, I still think that it's close to a scam. They say that if liberal arts grads choose a sales job, the employment rate is high. If so, what's needed is not academic ability but communication skills; Japan on the whole would get on fine if people went to technical high schools and schools to develop communication skills. I blew it. So, I thought that I would get it back with this job."

It is a very extreme argument but there is strong persuasive power and sound reasoning in what Mori says. And in interviewing him, I recalled an interview that I conducted several years before. Actually, it was around the time of the Lehman shock, when I had begun interviews to research the subject of the increase in the number of college graduates working in shady businesses, that I had to endure lecturing from young people who were hired by loan sharks immediately after graduating college. This is what they said:

"Mr. Suzuki, do you think that the guys who go to college are all from wealthy families? At the university I went to, there were lots of guys who weren't so smart, but their parents borrowed money to put them in school. So after graduating they all went to repay their parents. Not only tuition but even the pocket money they were sent. Not everybody couldn't find a job or became NEET[27] after graduation."

This speech is recorded in the book I was writing at that time; I took them as words coming from a juvenile delinquent who had been raised in an extremely poor family. "I can't believe that someone would go to high school and then become a juvie" (he had read one of my books). His background was that he had borrowed money from a student loan company to pay for his living expenses while he was in college and was saddled with debt; as a result, he was recruited to work in loan sharking in the illegitimate section of a small consumer loan company to pay off his debts.

A few months after Mori had joined an "It's me!" scam cell, he repaid his mother's debts but even afterwards he maintained his relationship with the people in the cell as a spot player (who works when called).

"As a player, I'm just third-rate, and don't bring in much

[27] Not in Education, Employment, or Training.

compared to the other guys, but what I thought after learning about the world of fraud is that money makes the world go round. The guys who don't have money give up their own future because of money; from the start, they're not thinking about the future; they're just satisfied with what they've got. They're wimps who naturally quit too soon. I'm balancing being afraid and wanting a future, and I want to come out at the best spot. I believe it when they say that we won't be arrested. My mom would really cry if I was arrested."

4.5 Case 4: Born in an overwhelmingly poverty-stricken area

Chikushi Taiga. He was born in 1992 and grew up in a mountainous area of a prefecture in southern Japan. He was the only son of a Japanese mother and an American GI stationed in a large city in central Japan. His parents divorced when he was in elementary school and his mother moved to her hometown in a mountainous area. They lived in a dilapidated house on his grandmother's property; it was so dilapidated that during a heavy rain, "it would rain into the house" (because there were large holes in the walls).

It was certainly a region where "delinquency culture" thrived; from elementary school he stole tobacco from his classmate's tobacco farm and smoked it, or he would steal a motor scooter parked on the road for joyrides. However, it was a mountain village with a very small population and very easygoing, so nobody locked their motor scooters; even if he stole one, if he left it parked nearby, nobody minded. However, there were very strict vertical relationships in the local delinquent society, so in junior high school, he couldn't even ride a remodeled scooter without his seniors' permission.

After graduating from junior high school and disliking the cooped-up feeling of the local delinquent society, he decamped to the nearby hub city with 100,000 yen in cash. He began working as a scout for the sex trade with other delinquents of his age group that he met in that city, and he even summoned the most spirited of his friends from his hometown. Through the introduction of a gangster who was looking out for him at that time, he gained experience as a withdrawer in the collection division of an early -stage fraud organization dealing in unlisted shares. He was arrested but the case was dropped; after that, he went to Tokyo and made his debut as an "It's me!" remittance scam player.

From about 2013 the number of men from the provinces who were players in scam cells or on their periphery began to increase. I heard people in the business speak of groups of bagmen, and even cell players, that were named after places, such as the F group (Tokyo and environs), the A group (Kanagawa Prefecture), the K group (southern Japan), the I group (remote islands), etc.

It had been my impression that, until then, most of the players who made up the core of the cells were from Tokyo or its environs; if there were any people from the provinces they were used just as bagmen. Following the entry of juniors of metropolitan semi-gangsters (non-officially designated organized-crime groups) who had been engaged in loan-sharking, men with backgrounds in legitimate businesses, and college graduate players, the power of men from the provinces became conspicuous ten years after this remittance scam first appeared.

Chikushi was a member of the K group, one of those that I had heard about. What was surprising in what he said was his description of his hometown.

"Everybody in the neighborhood was poor as dirt, really pinched. I'd hardly ever seen anybody who was well-off. If there was somebody like that, they'd have a store that'd been doing business in the area for generations. The whole area was rock-bottom poor and there weren't many people, so can you guess what happens? If a typhoon or even just a small storm comes, first of all, the whole place has a blackout and the power doesn't come back on for hours. If we're unlucky, it won't come back for half a day. Besides that, there's only one convenience store in the area, so before a typhoon comes the local people buy up everything so there's no food or anything left on the shelves, and the place is empty. Then, because there's no electricity, the alarms and security cameras aren't working so we used to go and rob the convenience store lots of times when a typhoon came. There was money there. But we did it so many times that they put in a safe."

It is hard for us to imagine, but H Town, where Chikushi grew up, was such a place. The local industry did not decline; it never grew in the first place. The main industries were agriculture and raising livestock but there was no specialization. As a matter of course, the population was aging and shrinking more and more; as a result, it was becoming a so-called marginal settlement. However, because it had good access by a national highway to the neighboring areas and the hub city (although the city itself was some distance away), quite a few households with young children remained. Because the land was on a steep slope, housing development was on a very small scale; on the other hand, for some reason, there was some old public housing in the town. I investigated this and found that it was built in the mid-Showa period (1950s–1960s) for people employed in this region's forestry industry and at a small hydroelectric power plant.

It is said that the scene of Japan's rural areas today is the same everywhere, but this town had no roadside business complex with a large supermarket, used bookstores, and recycle shops located in one large site, nor did it have an AEON mall;[28] there wasn't even a pachinko parlor. It is almost unimaginable.

"Even so, the old people in my hometown are something else. Some of them are on welfare or something, but there's a waiting list. The town is poor as dirt, so it can't take care of all the people who ask for welfare, so there's a waiting list. It seems that when one old person on welfare dies, the next old guy can get it.

"But the real reason the old people are something else is that they can manage to eat even if there's no work. What

[28] The AEON MALL Co. constructs large shopping malls in many areas of Japan.

I mean is that the old folks are farming their own land, behind their houses or off in the mountains, so they can pretty much feed themselves. And because of that the old guys and the old women too are really brawny with thick arms; it's really scary. My grandma is especially scary.

"For example, when I was a kid, we would steal stuff from somebody's field, make a campfire in the mountains, and eat it. Then my grandma would come after us with a sickle, and throw all of us over her shoulder. When you're thrown onto the hard ground, it really knocks the breath out of you. She would say, 'If you're so hungry, just say so,' and would stamp off into the mountains. What do you think she would do? She'd come back with a rabbit or some critter that she had caught. Then we would dress it and eat it."

There are no misprints in the above profile. He is Japanese, born in 1992. It is surprising that such an area exists in Japan but even more surprising are the profiles of the grandparents of Chikushi and his friends who are involved in fraud at present. Concerning the grandmother who threw the local kids over her shoulder and wiped them out, and then hunted wild animals, if we trace back, we find that she was a war orphan from the Second World War. I do not know what path she took to arrive at this town, but it must have involved great suffering and many vicissitudes.

On the other hand, the grandfather of Chikushi's friend K, who is working at present in the same fraud cell, had been a bandit who made his living by attacking people who were walking on the roads in his district. This seems inconceivable to us today.

"I didn't have any money when I was a kid, but I still had a good time, more or less. As soon as I entered junior high, we'd descend on the junior highs in neighboring towns one after the other and challenge the strongest guy they had to a fight. For some reason, in my hometown junior high they trained us just in martial arts from the time we were kids, so I had confidence in my ability. And then they did the same thing in junior highs here and

there, and, as you'd expect, that led to juvie seniors crop-
ping up. The relationships are made there, but my
hometown was that kind of place from way back; the
same kind of messed up seniors going way back in succession, just loafing around."

I wrote above that his seniors' permission was needed
even to ride a scooter; in Chikushi's hometown it was said
that "the seniors' words are the voice of heaven"; absolute
obedience was required and there were frequent punishments. Having grown up in such a place, Chikushi made a
big decision when he graduated from junior high school.

"My friends and I asked each other what we were going
to do after graduation. The guys whose parents had money were going to high school, but we didn't have that
option, so one of my friends from the same H Town said,
'We were born and brought up in our parents' town, so
thanks to that, what can we do but become yakuza?'
Otherwise, we'd get a local job and live poor as dirt. Well,
we'd be poor, but we'd have our local friends; it wouldn't
be any fun to go off to work in the hub city, would it?
That's the kind of things they were saying. They were
what you call 'mild *yankī*.' I hated that, so I ripped off the
cash register at a gas station and with the 100,000 yen I
got, I took off for F City, the biggest in the prefecture."

There he connected with a new group of delinquents
and found work as a scout for the sex industry and immediately sent for several friends from his hometown and
assigned them jobs. However, after he made quite a lot of
money, he was pressured by a local gangster into joining
his gang. He didn't want to do that so with the interven-
tion of a different gangster he came to the Kanto region
to work as a bagman for an unlisted shares fraud. There
Chikushi and the others, being natives of H Town, experienced a shock.

"What surprised me was how soft the Tokyo outlaws
are. We were told to be withdrawers, and that means the
staff who get arrested. Naturally, you do it many times and
you'll be arrested again and again, but in the end, they
drop the charges. Then after that we would go to the top

123

guy and ask for the next job. Then he said, 'You guys have already been arrested once for withdrawing so do you really want to do it again? Usually guys quit after one arrest.' We were surprised and couldn't understand his meaning. But I suppose that's the Tokyo people's way of thinking. We didn't intend to be disposables. We asked him to give us better jobs too and that was our start as players. We didn't get any training, we just showed up at the cell where we were supposed to work and were told to come back when we'd memorized the script."

Was it just that they had more guts? To those like Chikushi, who had been brought up on the rule that "the seniors' words are the voice of heaven," the rule in the scam cells of absolute obedience to the leaders was nothing like real absolute obedience and easy to put up with, and as players they soon were taking in large amounts of money.

This income was then returned to their hometowns. The way it worked was that for anyone who was willing, those of the same age or juniors, they would pay their fares and bring them to Tokyo, and rent apartments where they could live. Those with strong motivation were trained as scam players, and those who wanted just to make a killing and return to their hometown were given collection work. Chikushi and his friends took a certain percentage of their earnings as a kickback. This was the background of the K group; in other words, they formed a dispatch agency supplying scammers.

"We have some exchanges with groups that come from other regions, and those guys mostly have backgrounds similar to ours. What's funny is that in their hometowns too they've got the tradition of 'the seniors' words are the voice of heaven.' When we bring some guys with high motivation from our hometown, the leaders probably think that we're of some use. We don't care who we might take money from. We just take from guys who have money. The juvies in Tokyo say, 'I'll do anything but murder,' but to us that's laughable; if there's money in it we'd kill somebody. That's because if you stay at home without doing anything, or if you go back home without accomplishing anything, you'll wind up as a yakuza who can't make a living your whole life. If you run an honest business in our hometown, you can barely make a living however hard you try. On the other hand, if you leave home and run an honest business, you'll be even worse off, and you also have to pay rent. In the end, if illegal is the only choice, there's no difference between grey and pitch black. So we went completely black. That's all there is to say."

In Chikushi's description, the area where he was brought up is very different from the typical Japanese scene, and his motivation sounds less like that of an illegal business operator and more like a "delinquent foreigner."

I want to consider here the tremendous sense of distance between Chikushi and his friends, and the wealthy elderly people from whom they are now taking money. The feelings that Chikushi and his friends have are very close to the sense of distance felt by the farmers and burghers who brought about the bourgeois revolutions of early modern Europe from the aristocrats living in their walled castles. For Chikushi and his friends, the wealthy elderly live in a completely different social class that they cannot even imagine. On the one hand, Chikushi says dreadful things like, "If there's some old guy that we know has several tens of millions of yen in his house, we'd take it even if we have to kill him and burn down his house," yet he takes very good care of his hometown friends and looks after his juniors attentively; he is warm-hearted and would never betray anyone. For them, the elderly who hoard money are in a different sphere, not even human.

These young people are the products of Japan's polarized society, or rather, of Japan's rigid class society.

4.6 What we can learn from these four cases

What do you think? These are the backgrounds of the young people who are living in the sites of fraud. Considering the composition of players as a whole, types such as Kanbe and Chikushi are numerous but the other two examples were listed to introduce the distinguishing features of their motivation. In any case, there are no children of good families here, but on the other hand, there are no outlaws with a weak understanding of what it means to be law-abiding, who dirtied their hands with fraud partly in fun.

Meeting them face-to-face, I felt that the common point in the interviews was their economic resentment. But this is probably a point shared in common by almost everyone who engages in crime. What I felt even more strongly was that, compared to the average person of the same generation, they were extremely grown-up and mature as human beings. Leaving aside however much they had been trained at scam cells, they had motivation that could only be described as too much or too intense.

Concerning their mental age, I felt particularly about players like Kanbe (Case 1) and Chikushi (Case 4), who had risen from the ranks of genuine delinquents, that in comparison to average people of their generation, or even comparing them to delinquents who lived in worlds other than the fraud business, they clearly were much more composed, thought things through carefully, had made a habit of deliberating carefully before acting, and despite their youth, hardly displayed an impulsive side. Further, even though they had dirtied their hands with fraud, which is generally thought to be an inhuman and evil crime, on the other hand they are considerate of their friends and choose to put kindness before profit.

Chikushi not only made a hobby out of nurturing his juniors but during the time he was earning the most as a player he sent to his mother at home 1,200,000 yen every month, and brought his grandmother, the one who hunted critters, to Tokyo and took her around sightseeing.

Do scam cells really nurture people to that extent? Is this an escape from a place where everyone is always tense? We can say of their personalities that despite their careless language and mischievous expressions, they are mature beyond their years.

Concerning their excessive motivation, I feel that they

are the heretics of their generation. Recently, I have a strong sense of a trend in which the mild *yankī* personality is developing not only in regional cities but is reaching even to undergraduates in the capital; they have no ambition to succeed, have no prospects for the future, but are satisfied with the status quo and just living with their friends. This is the so-called "enlightened generation," but in that same generation, even at the stage before joining a scam cell, they already were displaying motivation so high it might be called heretical.

They probably cannot act with a group if the bonds are loose. Their personalities are such that, within a relaxed status quo community, they cannot avoid seeming out of place, so people would say of them, "What's that guy glaring at?" or "He's so cringe!" It is just because they are like that that they have a strong sense that a scam cell was the place that they belonged, cells being groups with firm rules and upward mobility.

This is my frank impression. I believe that they are people of ability who would have made great achievements if they had become eager company employees during Japan's postwar period of high economic growth. They are young people of truly outstanding quality, with strong convictions and the ability to act, men who are in fact well-honed blades.

However, they are heretics. However much they strive, however much they race vigorously, leaving the others behind, there is no guarantee of compensation or a future corresponding to that effort in the legitimate businesses of today. They are alienated from the community of those of the same generation who have the status quo type of motivation, being told, "You're the only one out of step." To them, those who tend to depravity, the scam cells seem to be a shining light.

The scam cells, which are aberrant groups, satisfy greatly their feelings of being helpless and isolated. Or rather, this might be the result of fraud organizations having sought methods of gathering and training the most outstanding players, as they became more highly sophisticated.

127

Chapter 5

Who gave birth to those who prey on the elderly? Traces of Japanese society's underside

5.1 Are those who prey on the elderly antiheroes?

The appearance of young people who prey on the elderly was inevitable within Japan's relentlessly distorted class society. Therein was located what might be called "under-the-table redistribution." They themselves describe this as their justification. They feel refreshed just because those words clearly present a sound argument.

However, are they really the antiheroes of the present age? Can they, who have experienced scam cells, escape that business and become the youthful leaders of the (underground) economy? That can hardly be the case because preying on the elderly after all is an underground business, and hence illegal.

A decade after special fraud crimes had begun to sweep across Japan, the fraud enterprise underwent a major change around 2013. Returning to the narrative, let us take a look at what happened. The Kato group's scam cells will again appear in this final story. What has happened to Kurusu, the 23-year-old who had recently been promoted to the status of cell manager? What happened with the previously unheard-of project of opening six scam cells simultaneously, with Dokugawa promoted to sub-*bantō*?

Kurusu, who was promoted from a regular player to cell manager on the occasion of the opening of six new cells simultaneously, a rare event in the world of fraud, was completely exhausted by the fifth day of operations.

Until now, Dokugawa had been his immediate superior, but Dokugawa had left the cell and was now supervising three cells as a sub-*bantō*, working under the *bantō* Kato.

Kurusu was given a cell office, eight players including three new and five experienced players, a 400-item name list, and shuffled cell phones. Using these resources, he had been ordered to achieve a take quota of 120 million yen in the one month that the short-term cell would operate.

However, in the first place, the setup itself was unusual, and an atmosphere of dissatisfaction soon began to spread among the experienced players. Shortly after the cell opened, Shindō, a player slightly older than Kurusu, came up to tell him, "Something's not right here." He was a mid-level player with one year's experience. Until just the other day he had used peer language with Kurusu, but since Kurusu had been promoted to cell manager, Shindō had begun to use polite language to him. "Let's see. First of all, the name list is too small. If we pick up the pace, 400 items won't last us even a week."

There was good reason for Kurusu to be at his wit's end. Usually, in making scam calls, the person being called is not necessarily at home, or, suspecting a fraud, the called person hangs up fairly quickly; for these reasons, the work of making the phone calls itself does not take so much time. During the time the office can be used, a name list of 2,000 items would not be enough for three teams; however, their list had only 400 names. Further, they had been given a quota.

"Don't worry about the deadline for closing the office and that stuff; the point is that we've got confidence in the quality of this name list. Actually, the feeling of using a fresh name list gives a completely different reaction. There're lots of marks who're gaga here, and I've got the feeling that they have money. It's a sure thing that these 400 names will get us more than a hundred million yen."

"I see…"

In fact, as Shindō said, there was something different about this name list and Kurusu felt the same. Actually, on the fifth day, they made some money. There were seven hits on the fifth day, coming to a total of 16,000,000 yen. This hit ratio was not common.

However, they had already called a large number of the names on the list and their quota was ten times what they had taken in. In just a short time they would use up the name list; if they could not do better than that, it would appear that Kurusu did not have what it took to be a cell manager.

"I'll go and talk to Dokugawa. We'll probably change the plan of action from next week, so I'll call a meeting the first thing in the morning."

"Please do that." Shindō said this with a blank look, increasing Kurusu's sense of panic.

5.2 Use it down to the dregs

Late at night, Dokugawa, the new sub-*bantō*, arrived at the meeting place and surprisingly, he was grinning. He had already received a report about the situation in the cell. Kurusu, thinking that he surely would be scolded, felt relieved, but also had an ominous feeling, suspecting that there was something behind that smile.

"Hi! Have you eaten?"

"I can't swallow anything. I haven't eaten since noon."

"Oh, no, you've got to eat. There's probably some place around here without cameras that's open late at night. Let's talk while we eat."

Dokugawa took him firmly by the arm. He was extremely cautious while the cells were in operation, especially disliking surveillance cameras, and even wore a mask[29] when he went to buy something at a convenience store. The place they entered was a nearby Korean barbecue restaurant under private management.

After they had ordered the usual items, Dokugawa questioned Kurusu with a laugh.

"Well? What do you think you should do?"

"First, should I change the script to raise the take on each hit, or improve the hit rate itself? With the three-player, out-of-court settlement type that we're using now,

[29] Even before the pandemic, Japanese people commonly wore surgical masks in public places to avoid catching or spreading colds, etc. and as a preventive measure against hay fever.

it's really tough to get more than three million per hit, however hard you try. Besides that, we can narrow down the hits to those who are gaga and have money, and we'll go back to them several times to the tune of several tens of millions. Right now, we have seven hits, so we can really sink our teeth into them."

"I see! And what about the name list?"

"It's amazing! I really get the feeling from their reactions that we can scam them."

When the elderly waitress, who seemed less than motivated, brought their meat, Kurusu lowered his voice. But Dokugawa somehow looked satisfied.

"Very good! If you had said something like 'Give me more name lists,' I would have socked you one."

"Really?" Kurusu, who had been thinking of that as one of the worst options, felt greatly relieved. However, as he heard what Dokugawa was saying, his feeling of tension returned.

"This time we set a quota of more than 100 million yen but that was just something to aim for. Sorry about that. We just wanted to try you out. Don't tell anybody in the cell. The other cells are really making money so at this cell do it your way and get the biggest take that you can. With the same script and the same method that you've been using, the name list will be used up in just a few days, right? After you've finished it, if you come to ask me what to do, you'll get a beating just for that. If I have to tell you every little thing, you'll never improve."

"Really?"

Was this cell just to try Kurusu out? Of course, things weren't that lenient, but just because he understood that they had high hopes for him made him feel motivated.

"Then, what do you think of my strategy?"

"It's good on the whole. With the three-player, out-of-court settlement script that you're using, the best thing is to really stick it to the ones who are gaga. There're quite a few, aren't there?"

"There sure are! There are even old ladies who just keep saying 'Please forgive me!' from the time we call until we hang up."

"Just as I thought! It'll be OK just to focus on those and aim for four hits of 30 million yen over the month. That's the easy way. However, ..." Dokugawa' changed his tone of voice.

"Kurusu, is that really OK with you? With such a great name list, is it really OK to shoot 396 blanks out of 400?"

Of course it is not. That would be a significant loss. The name list they are using is the name list broker's best quality. What is demanded of the cell players is to use this name list to the full, grinding it into powder as they turn it into cash. Kurusu understood that very well.

As Kurusu thought that over silently, a file was smacked down in front of him.

"This is a collection of the one-shot scripts that we've used up to now. Check these against the name list that you're using now and think up the best plan by yourself."

"The name list too?"

"Hey, why do you think that the name list has an evaluation column? If you call up and just say hello, nothing's gonna happen, right?"

The name lists include a number of categories supplied by the augmenters' surveys. In addition to basic information such as age, sex, address, etc., there is information on the degree of senility, whether or not they have nursing care, how much money they keep at home, etc.

Paying no attention to his meat, Kurusu studied the file while sub-*banto* Dokugawa gazed at him with satisfaction.

5.3 A hand-written "threatening scenario"

The next morning, among the players who as usual were all present before the 8:00 am starting time, there were a few who appeared dissatisfied. The reason was that today was not supposed to be a workday. At first, Kurusu had established a five-day work week because of the small number of names on the name lists, but late at night on the previous day he had summoned everyone on their business phones.

Kurusu glared at them. "Sorry about today but I got you

here because I've got something I want to say to you. From today, the policy of our cell will change completely, both the scripts and the team makeup. Because, in fact, we're really going to aim at 120 million yen."

Apparently, he had spent the night poring over the materials without sleeping. His eyes were bloodshot, but his words revealed his strong will. Listening to him, the players became energized.

"If we change the scripts, what'll we do about training?"

"I've asked for a coach to come tomorrow. I'll pay the cost out of my own pocket. I'm betting that our take will go up even if I pay for two- or three-day's training."

Even the experienced players had never heard of a cell manager paying for additional training out of his own pocket. If the cost of training was 20,000 yen per person, Kurusu was going to hand over 180,000 yen for one day, and 540,000 yen if the training went to three days. The players could see his determination.

"Specifically, from today we're going to divide into three teams that will follow different plans. First, team number one will target the seven hits we've had up to now and keep sticking it to them with threats. You don't need any training for that! Keep threatening them."

"if we threaten them, won't they go to the police?"

This question was only natural, but Kurusu handed all of them a sheet of paper. It was Kurusu's handwritten "threatening scenario."

"No problem if they go to the police. Use a different script to deceive the family. The point is to go as far as saying 'If you don't pay up, we'll burn down your house or kill somebody. Our gang's pretty big so even if somebody is arrested, we'll definitely take revenge.' If necessary, it's OK to say something like 'You went to the police and thanks to that, one of us was arrested and is in trouble, so pay us compensation.'" Find out how much they can pay and make them pay the max."

An outrageous, over-the-top idea but in the end, it strikes at the psychology of the victims, who fear the revenge of an invisible criminal organization, and it could bring about a "fever." Already, several of the players looked as if they belonged on this team. This was the type of player who liked bullying and swindling; in the cells they were called the "ultra-scammers."

What were the other two teams going to do? Kurusu told everyone to take another look at the name list they had been using.

"I have been looking at this name list all night and I think that it's tops. These 400 names are, all of them, every one, the names of old people living alone, and the names of their deceased husbands or wives, their date of death, and even the names of their former employers are all listed. We can use this, absolutely. Anybody know the deceased person scam that was common a few years ago?"

Shindō, the player who had spoken to Kurusu yesterday after working hours, seemed to know it. "That's the one where you demand repayment of money that you loaned to the dead guy before he croaked."

"That's it. Have you ever seen a name list with this kind of detailed information about the deceased? Probably not. This is a gold mine because they can't check up with a guy who's dead. There're lots of ways to play it—he owes me money is a good one, or he kept a woman and has an illegitimate kid, and she's strapped for cash or needs money for child support, or she wants consolation money, or it's been discovered that he embezzled a lot of money from his former company and they're going to file a complaint unless the mark makes an out-of-court settlement. For these, you can do it solo or in teams of two; it looks like we've got the scripts for these so from tomorrow we'll start training."

Using these scripts is possible just because the material consists of very detailed personal information about the deceased.

Just then, someone asked permission to speak. It was a new recruit named Gōriki. "Is it OK to ask a question?"

"What?"

"This name list shows how much cash they keep at home, doesn't it?"

In fact, unbelievably, there were many cases with notations like "50 million yen in cash and 20 million in securities."

"And it also shows the level of nursing care they need. So, supposing we use an out-of-court settlement script and lure them out. They'll have to call one of those wheelchair-accessible taxis and while they're out, we could just break in. How about that?"

In an instant, the office fell silent. Of course. You could say by phone that the person who will receive the out-of-court settlement has been delayed and drag things out. One or two hours would be enough to steal the wealth hidden at home.

"I don't mean to brag, but I have several old juvie friends who were good at that and said absolutely that they would do it for a percentage. It would be too cruel to take everything, so they should leave enough so that the old guy won't starve."

It sounded convincing. However, if they used Gōriki's friends, and those friends were caught in the act, there was the risk that that would lead the police investigation from Gōriki to the cell.

"I see. I'll ask the people at the top what they think, and if it's OK we should go for it."

Hearing what Kurusu said, Gōriki made a slight winner's pose. It was only natural for if they were able to take 100 million yen, Gōriki's pay for the day would be 10 million. It was only natural that he would get fired up.

"OK, let's go!" That shout broke out somewhere. Seeing that the players' enthusiasm had returned, Kurosu thought, 'With these guys, it's all about cash.'

Actually, managing the players' motivation was more difficult than he had thought. They were guaranteed a daily payment of 20,000 yen under the name of transportation expenses, whether a scam succeeded or not. If everyone feels that their scams are failing, they fall into a low-energy mode and lose their motivation. However, if they make a hit, their share is about 10%, so as a matter of course their daily take would come to 200,000 or 500,000 yen.

If the hits are infrequent, what happens is that they fall into a way of thinking like playing pachinko aimlessly, hoping that they might get a hit. Naturally, the take will go down and they are likely to fall into a negative spiral. However, this time, they somehow were able to pull out of that spiral. Kurusu's determination was renewed.

5.4 A problem arises

The cell had been operating for two weeks. Dokugawa, seeing the income figures, rolled his eyes in surprise. The six cells had an average take of 50 million yen. It seemed that these name lists were no ordinary ones. But that was not the problem. The take of the new manager Kurosu's cell, which was supposed to be in training, was a mind-blowing 86 million yen.

"What a change! This is beyond expectations." Without realizing it, Dokugawa was talking to himself as he drove; he was feeling depressed.

In fact, a problem had arisen.

As sub-*bantō*, Dokugawa managed three cells. His most important task as *bantō* was to direct the collection of the money. In the Kato group of cells, when one team succeeded in a scam, the cell manager reported it to the *bantō*, who then sent the detailed information to A group (a collection group that collected the money from the victim directly). A would use three levels of messengers, B, C, and D, to finally hand the money to the *bantō*. The *bantō*, as the information hub, constantly wore a Bluetooth earbud to be able to get reports of success from the cells at any moment. Just this made this job very demanding. The *bantō* would then distribute the money, finally delivering the remaining amount to the backer; however…

Because his three cells were simultaneously using high quality name lists, a completely unexpected situation occurred: a failure to collect the take because of a shortage of bagmen. By the second week, even if a report from a cell arrived and the A shop was contacted, on several occasions all of the bagmen were out on other collections.

Even though the working cells had gone to great pains to succeed in a scam, if the ones who are to collect the money cannot collect it at just the right time, the take is lost. The reason is that if A group sets out at a leisurely pace, several hours after the scam call or the next day, the risk becomes much greater that during that time the police will go into action by staking out the place where the money is to be handed over. As a result of this problem, the losses (the amount that could not be collected) of the three cells managed by Dokugawa came to 20 million yen.

In a dark mood, Dokugawa nosed his car into a large home improvement store's parking lot, where Kato's car was parked in front of him. In fact, to carry out the work of a *bantō*, Kato, like Dokugawa, was wearing an earbud.

Kato, seeing that Dokugawa had arrived, got into his car's passenger's seat.

"Hi! Kurusu's cell is really something! We'll have to give him the Golden Arrow Award."[30]

Kato spoke excitedly but he himself as a player had attained an annual income of more than 40 million yen (total loss to the victims of over 400 million yen). However, the present-day situation was completely different. The amount of losses from fraud reported by the police continued to increase steadily but this showed only that the number of players and cells was growing, and the amount taken in each hit was getting higher. For the take of a new manager's cell to rise to over 160 million yen on a monthly basis showed immense power.

However, Dokugawa was not completely happy about it.

"We're in a bind... Actually, at Kurusu's cell, properly speaking, there's still nine million uncollected. When I got the report, A didn't have the staff... The same thing is happening at the other cells, so speaking frankly, I'm out 20 million."

There was no point in keeping it secret. Dokugawa sum-

[30] The Golden Arrow Award was awarded by the Japan Magazine Publishers Association (JMPA) to recognize excellence in Japan's media.; one category was "Best Newcomer."

moned up his courage and spoke but Kato's reaction was just, "Oh, yeah?"

"Is this OK? Isn't it a huge loss?"

"Well, to tell you the truth, I'm in the same spot and I'm already out 30 million."

"Really! Well, let's get on the ball and get some replacements for A. The way I see it, adding just four more bagmen would do the trick."

It was a natural expansion of facilities, but Kato frowned.

"About that… It's kind of a problem. We're talking big money here, right? And one of the backers is saying that he'll introduce some people to A, but…"

Wasn't this a godsend? Dokugawa could not understand why Kato was so worried, but there was a reason.

"I don't know that guy very well, but he is a 100% gangster (yakuza). What do you think? If somebody we don't know introduces someone to A, there's a chance that he will take off with the money. Originally, there's the risk of having to chase after A himself if he runs off with the money, but that becomes much worse if they're guys introduced by a yakuza. And if we get replacements for A from somewhere else, that yakuza will be complaining that we refused his men and got someone else's."

"A yakuza? Even so, shouldn't you accept even temporarily? With A shorthanded, our losses will continue. It's frustrating, and its absolutely inefficient. Generally speaking, if one of the bagmen absconds, isn't it logical that the one who makes up the loss is the yakuza who introduced him?"

"Dokugawa, you don't know the yakuza. If a guy could be made to do that, he wouldn't be a real yakuza."

Kato was not eager to do it, but it was certain that he would lose face with the players who have been working hard in the cells if they continued to fail to collect in this way, after taking so much trouble to set up this system. Further, if the players could not get their share after succeeding in a scam because of a failure to collect, it was within the bounds of possibility that they would confront the *bantō* himself.

From Dokugawa's point of view, who, as a newly appointed sub-*banto*, was aiming at becoming a *bantō* in the future, this would be a severe blemish on his career. Dokugawa appealed to the vacillating Kato.

"It'll be OK. Let's accept his offer. If they can't make the collections, it's a complete loss, but if they can actually collect the money then whatever happens it just becomes a question of dividing it up, doesn't it?"

"You think so? Another thing that we could do is not tell the players that the collection failed and just keep the secret among the *bantō*."

"I'm out 20 million. With three players on a team, their take is six million, so will I have to take the loss?"

"Hmm. I'm thinking more and more that it would be great if the collection team we have now could make the collections. It's really a terrible waste."

After thinking silently for a while, Kato slapped his knee as if he had made up his mind.

"OK! Let's go with this proposal. After it's settled, I'll send you the contact information of the new A leader. What a pain in the neck! Why did this have to happen? I thought that scams would go more smoothly; I feel as if I'd like to go back to being a just a player."

Hearing Kato grumble like this, Dokugawa looked at him in surprise. If you continue as a *bantō* for a long time, you meet conflicts and troubles beyond what he had imagined.

5.5 A decision that backfired in the worst way

However, Kato's gloomy premonition came true. Kato and Dokugawa's decision backfired in the worst way.

To begin with, the A group introduced by that backer imposed an unheard-of condition of 25% as the collection fee. That is, for a scam that took ten million yen, the collection group's take was 2.5 million yen. In return, as a special service, in addition to the messengers from A to B and C forming one set, a mysterious service was added in which the money was laundered. To prevent a situation in which the serial numbers, fingerprints, etc. on the bills received from the victim were checked by the police so they could be traced when the bills were used later, the bills collected were replaced with different bills.

Things weren't clear, but they had no choice. However, seven days after they started using this A group for collections, an incident occurred.

Staff member B, the messenger from this A group to the *bantō*, was assaulted and robbed of all of the money he was carrying. To make matters worse, the amount of the take was nine million yen. It was the take of Kurusu's cell.

The night that this happened, Kato and Dokugawa were summoned to an apartment in Tokyo.

"Well, what are you going to do about this?"

The man threatening them in a hoarse voice was the one who had looked at Kato with cold eyes when Kato was summoned to the private room at the grilled meat restaurant at the time this project was launched. He was in his 50s and one finger of his left hand had been neatly cut off. One hundred people out of a hundred would say at once that he was pure yakuza.

"Well, practically speaking, there's nothing that we can do."

When Kato replied in this way, the man shouted in a threatening voice, "What the hell do you mean by that?"

In fact, up to now, doing nothing was the scam cells' policy.

"It's money from a scam. If the scam fails, we've got zero. We think of it as money that we never had from the beginning. Generally speaking, if we lay the blame on someone and hound him, he's likely to suddenly turn against us and spill his guts to the cops, so everyone will be arrested. Basically, our policy up to now has been that if someone is knocked around, we give that person a little compensation and forget about it."

Unquestionably, considering the safety of the group, this is the best thing to do. However, this man didn't accept that logic.

"It was the guy who I introduced that got attacked!

Who could have done that?"

What this man was trying to say was this: the only ones who knew that A was going to collect from the victim were the people connected to the cell. Didn't that mean that someone connected to the cell had A followed and ambushed B, the messenger who collected the money? In other words, the guilty person was one of the players in Kurusu's cell, where the order to collect the money came from.

"It wouldn't be anyone from the cell. Usually, if B is ambushed, it's by somebody B knows, or B is just pretending to be attacked, or the ambush was done by A or C, the only people in contact with B."

"How can you be so sure?"

"Because there's no advantage for anybody in a cell to attack the likes of a bagman. The presence of a trouble-maker who would do something like that would bring the police down on the cell. All of them know that plugging away at making a score is both profitable and safe."

"Listen, kid! Don't give me such twisted talk!" the man shouted, and threw an ashtray at Kato. This was a typical scene from a straight-to-video gangster film.

"Anyhow, you'd better have the guys in that cell cough up the money!"

"I can't do that."

When Kato replied in this way the man didn't throw an ashtray but slapped Kato's face hard.

"Don't you give me any lip! I'll grant you that you too, as well as my side, which lost the money, are down. But the kid from my group got knocked down and beaten like hell. While he was on his motorbike he was hit by a car, knocked over, and beaten to a pulp with a metal bat. So you've gotta do your share about his medical expenses and consolation money."

"So what are you saying that we should do?"

"I'll wait until the weekend but show up with nine million yen to clear your debt."

"....."

"Did you hear me? "I'll cut you down right here!"

It was Kato who wanted to cut somebody down but still bleeding at the nose, he had to put up with it. All he could do was take his leave.

"I understand."

In the end, Dokugawa at his side did not say a word, but just hung his head, dumbfounded.

5.6 Their decision

In the end, the *banto* Kato took responsibility for this situation. By all rights, the management of this cell was Dokugawa's responsibility, but Kato insisted that he take responsibility alone, and so the matter was settled.

While descending the emergency stairs to the condo's parking lot, Kato was expressionless.

"Shit! For guys in the business to be called to a condo covered with security cameras! If we're caught, he's next in line. That guy is really clueless!"

Dokugawa's expression was dark as he spoke to Kato, who out of spite was pounding the banister as he descended. "I'm wondering if that attack wasn't a put-up job by that guy."

"Dokugawa, saying things like that will lead to a war."

Actually, this was in fact a delicate situation. If the backer and the *bantō* start to doubt each other, it will cause problems for business in the future.

"Mr. Kato, does this kind of thing happen often?"

"It never has before."

Unexpectedly, Kato stopped at the landing. "Mr. Dokugawa…"

"You're calling me 'Mr.'? Why?"

"I'll ask you again. I'm thinking that if you can learn the work of a *bantō* completely, I'll pull out. If so, you'll be the *bantō*. Is that OK?"

"Well… Why are you suddenly using polite language to me?"

"I'm serious. All the time I've been doing scams, the time when I was a player with you was the best. Sometimes we all went to the beach or someplace together."

Kato was looking straight ahead. At his words, Dokugawa's expression relaxed.

"So we did. In those days we weren't held so tightly. All the players went drinking together, and went to the beach, and once we smashed up a jet ski on some rocks."

Without their noticing it, their use of polite language had returned to its usual relationship.

Kato's talents had been recognized and he had been promoted to *bantō*, but his take in itself did not match Dokugawa's in the long run. Kato had the ability to gather people and motivate them, handle the business income and expenditures dependably, etc., and he was quick-witted, steady, and trustworthy. For these reasons he got ahead of Dokugawa, who was older, had more experience, and made higher earnings as a player. This was how Kato had become a *bantō*.

"Mr. Dokugawa, I'm asking you seriously. Is it really OK if I take off and dump everything on you?" Saying this, Kato stared fixedly.

For Dokugawa, too, this was a crucial moment.

"Kato, if you're asking me to do it, I'll do it. If you're saying that now is about the time for you to pull out, then do it. I'll take things over totally."

"Thank you."

Dokugawa felt for Kato, who bowed his head deeply.

The scam business is facing a period of sudden changes and turmoil. Becoming a *bantō* in the midst of those heavy seas means to protect the players, increase the profits, and gamble your whole life. So you wonder if you are up to it.

Around that time, Kurusu's cell was approaching the end of its cycle, and shouts of joy were being raised there. Kurusu had just announced the amount of that week's take. Some of the players had grown up in poverty. Some had uncontrollable motivation so strong it made them misfits. Some had always been despised as scum who could not do anything. However, by clinging to this place they were able to obtain money in amounts none of them had ever dreamed possible.

Liquor was forbidden so they made toasts with tea in plastic cups and that tea tasted better than even the most

143

expensive liquor. As he watched the players celebrating, Kurusu too again swore to himself that he would devote everything he had to this business.

5.7 The rapidly changing power relationships of scams

Originally, scams attracted people who were outlaws in loosely organized criminal groups but who did not belong to officially designated criminal organizations;[31] however, around 2013, the environment, power relationships, and structure changed rapidly. The fraud organizations began to be called with prefixes such as "A gang family," "B gang family," or "X group family." In other words, the fraud organizations became systematized. In the events related in Chapter 2, all of the backers assembled at the private room in the high-class grilled meat restaurant to which the *bantō* Kato was summoned, were men belonging to these groups.

However, when expressions such as "A family" began to appear at the scam cells, I, who had been continuing my data collection up to then, began to feel that something was wrong, because originally, scams and gangsterism were direct opposites.

One gang leader put it this way. "Basically, it goes by each family's policy, but scamming is forbidden as a yakuza business, because we're chivalrous groups that side with the weak and crush the strong.[32] The reason scamming became such a big business is that the gangs were not involved in it. Our organization is a family where the child supports the parent, and the parent gives work to the child, so a way of thinking that makes it normal to cut off the ones at the bottom is just not right. It's just for that reason that even if we have a similar form of organization, a loan-sharking organization that was very chival-

---

[31] On designation, see Reilly Jr. E. F. (2014). Criminalizing yakuza membership: A comparative study of the anti-boryokudan law. *Washington University Global Studies Law Review, 13*(4), 801-829, pp. 807-809. http://openscholarship. wustl.edu/law_globalstudies/vol13/iss4

[32] On the yakuza's chivalry, see Reilly, pp. 803-804.

rous would be exposed completely from top to bottom and collapse."

At any rate, that was the theory.

Why did the scam organizations become part of gangster families at this time? One who knew the circumstances was, after all, a former *bantō*. He served as the model for my description of the *bantō* Kato, and had this to say.

"It's just my guess but around the end of last year (2011) was when the Kantō Rengō and the Dragons (the two largest semi-gangster groups in the Kantō area) were designated as quasi-gangsters (*jun-bōryokudan*). I don't mean that these kinds of guys were backers but it's clear that around then many backers quit doing scams and moved into selling goods (the business of preying on the elderly with actual products—palming off fake goods such as health foods, etc.), so it was a time when the semi-gangster's money stopped flowing to the scam cells.

"We really felt that in the business as a whole, things were getting out of hand. Around that same time, two big tool dealers in Tokyo were caught and there was a shortage of tools so sometimes there was a real scramble for name lists and tools. On top of that, the name list of the targets that one cell has been on the point of scamming leaked, and some other cell used that name list on their own to pull a proxy refund claim (a method of fraud in which a service fee is taken for promising to return money stolen in a previous scam), so the first cell began a search, saying, 'If we find them, we'll kill them!'"

However sophisticated it may be, an underground business is an underground business. In the world of the scam organizations, internal frictions occur frequently. Naturally, whatever damage the people involved incur, they cannot file a report of damage with the police as in a criminal or civil case, so as a matter of course the ones who appear are the professional arbitrators of underground civil cases who have no connection with the police or lawyers, namely, the yakuza.

If there is friction between two organizations, they each get different yakuza for protection, and have them make a compromise. The model for the former *bantō* Kato continued:

"So then what happened was for that kind of trouble not to come up, affiliations were developed to some extent so as to better protect the name lists and tools in the future. Tokyo was divided up into four main groups. For convenience they were called the 'O family" or the 'X connection,' but in fact the members of those groups did not work as *bantō* or players. The main backer, the guy who advanced the largest amount of money among the backers, was not a designated gangster or a semi-gangster group member, and he didn't have to turn his take over to them. It's just that they would share people and materials within the same name and family, and any time there happened to be trouble with others they could make use of that name."

However, the yakuza and the semi-gangsters, who up to then basically had not been involved in the day-to-day operations of the scam organizations, hung out their shingles and drew the cells into their families, and the situation that had just been waiting to happen occurred. The law of competition arose among the various families. Each tried to be better than any other family-affiliated scam organization by collaring even more secure tools, even more thoroughly augmented name lists, and even more outstanding players.

It had been taken for granted that there was basically no interference within the business of the same fraud, even if there was trouble among some organizations; however, among those fraud organizations, a warring states period has now arrived.

5.8 Significant changes in the players' environment

The actual situation has proceeded much farther than in the above description. First, a big change occurred in the quality of the cell players and people in the collection agencies.

"For the cell players and the bagmen too, there's been an increase in the number of people who have been sent by people related to yakuza gangs. The yakuza are pros at recruiting people and swindling, aren't they? It's gotten so that people who are not actually enrolled as gang members but are always hanging round the fringes of the gangs, or those who were scam players years ago and are now placed on the edges, are brought in and taught the palaver and then sent to the cells. What that means is that a certain percent of what those players earn is taken by the guys who sent them. To give you a simple comparison, it's like the relationship between a scout and a sex worker, or a dispatch company and a temp. Another reason for this is that if one family's recruiter has got his teeth into a player, that prevents him from going to another family."

If we say that scams have become a source of income for the yakuza, what we imagine is that yakuza are in the position of the backer who is at the apex of the organization, and that the proceeds of the scam cells flow to the gangs as tribute, but that is not the case.

The backers' hands are clean, the *bantō* and players too are not registered gang members, but gang-affiliated persons recruit and deploy those players and bagmen and take a cut of their earnings, so from the yakuza's point of view, no great damage is done to their justification of chivalry, and they can get involved in that business. Depending on the number of people they deploy, it is possible that the yakuza can expect profits even greater than those of the backers.

If so, the competition for staff constantly heats up, and that is where things begin to come apart.

"Actually, even using the same name lists and scenarios, the take can differ as much as four times depending on the players. We're seeing the appearance of people like experienced players who have made a certain amount but don't leave the business, instead going to work someplace where the conditions are better. For example, at the X gang affiliates, they broke the standard rule of giving the players 10% of the take and raised it to between 15 and 30%. Or at the T gang affiliates, there's the policy of making outstanding players cell managers immediately and giving them their own cells. The aim is to increase the number of cells any way they can.

"But in fact, when it comes to this, however much the guys who shuffle the players around are under the yakuza's patronage, there'll always be some guys who are pulled out by another gang group. I've even heard of cell leaders who shuffled good players to another gang's affiliated cell and took a kickback. In the worst case, it happened that even if the guy who shuffles people is gang-connected, the take is completely different depending on the level of the cell that the guy was shuffled to, so he shuffled the guy again to a cell connected to a different gang."

This is a ludicrous situation. What he is saying is that a person affiliated with gang X, who is sending staff to a scam cell connected to gang X, is also sending players to a cell affiliated with gang Y, that supposedly is a competitor. This means that "affiliation" really has no meaning, and when disputes arise, things really get out of hand.

5.9 Unraveling born in the scam organizations

Cracks are beginning to appear in the hard-as-rock fraud organizations, which had appeared so solid as if there was no space for even a single razor blade to slide into. Attempting to gather players hastily leads to a decline in player quality, and acts of betrayal of the cells (such as fleeing with the take) also occur. Some scam organizations are even establishing limits on the number of players to cope with this decline in quality; however, as stated above, the take from the scams varies widely according to the quality of the players, so it is very difficult to gather only outstanding players.

Other problems were mounting as well. For example, there is the "BC jump." As stated above, in the fraud business recently, the collection divisions have been emerging as independent organizations, and their personnel is supplied by recruiters.

To review, the money collection route has been made complicated to protect the main fraud organization from exposure. As a result, for the sake of convenience, the bagmen groups who collect the cash directly from the victims on the spot are called A, the messenger groups who transport the take while covering their tracks are called B and C, and the ones who finally turn over the take to the cell *bantō* or manager are called D. Cases in which members of the B and C groups have been attacked by someone who stole the take, or who themselves took the money and disappeared, are called "BC jump." In fact, this happened in the narrative presented earlier in this chapter. In this kind of situation, the gang-affiliated recruiters who had dispatched the staff to the groups were at their wits' end.

"In cases like these, originally, you would say, 'bad luck' and forget about it but the affiliated gangs won't allow that. So the normal thing would be that the one who is forced to take the responsibility is the guy who sent people to A. The one put on the spot here is the guy who is shuffling players to the cells above the bagmen. But what do you think will happen when the guy who is sending people to A sends people who belong to a gang family different from the head organization family? Going after them will cause trouble between those gangs. On the other hand, even if they understand that they can't do that, there's the possibility that the top organization is plotting for the BC to jump be robbed. They'll start jumping at shadows, won't they? Doing that, they let down their guard, so next time even a cell will be attacked."

The scam cells boast of their iron wall of security against police investigations but, for example, if information that a large amount of cash is being held in the cell office the day before the players are to be paid is leaked to outsiders, that will invite robbers. Robbers are the fraud organizations' weakest point. If they put someone there as a watchman and he is beaten half to death, naturally they can never complain to the police. Wondering who tipped off the robbers leads to everyone doubting everyone else, and here cracks begin to appear in the absolute leadership of the *bantō* and cell manager.

For this reason in particular, players who could be trusted were required, and this led to the establishment of limits on the number of players, which in turn gave birth to a stalemate.

In this situation, the generation gap in the cell personnel puts additional pressure on the organization. I stated above that the energetic youth born in the provinces formed the main pool of personnel that lead the scam world at present. The sequence of events was that they used their contacts among local delinquents and their juniors, mobilizing large numbers of talented people and assigning them to the scam cells; however, to the highly motivated players in their early 20s, the present player candidates in their teens were overwhelmingly lukewarm. Chikushi, who was introduced in the previous chapter, was one who felt that way.

"The player candidates in their teens nowadays say really surprising things, like they'd rather be a bagman than a player. To tell the truth, as long as you're a player there's hardly any chance of being arrested. But the bagmen are disposable goods, it's just luck whether they're caught or not. But even if you tell them that, a lot of these kids still say that bagman is OK.

"The reason is that they just don't have any ambition. They're really mild *yankī* who think like migrant workers. If they can earn 500,000 yen, they want to go home and buy a used Vellfire. Or they'll say, 'If I could earn more, I'll get a Lexus,' adding 'My friends could never get one, could they?' A lot of those guys want to take weekends off, and in fact the number of cells closed on weekends is increasing. Some of the guys from my hometown are like that but the young guys from the Kanto area are really something else. The most hilarious guys are the J. League[33] supporters. 'I'll do anything for the Kashima Antlers! I'll put my life on the line!' They're just hopeless. Guys like this you can't use even for A (bagmen in the

---

[33] The Japan Professional Football [soccer] League; the Kashima Antlers are a professional football team based in Kashima City, Ibaraki Prefecture, in the Kanto area.

collection group) because when they're arrested, they'll probably spill their guts."

Previously, in Chikushi's group, the bagmen too were put up in a flophouse and fed until they had a job to do, and if they were arrested, they would be taken care of after their release. The best among them were trained so more than a few rose to become players.

"The bosses took care of everything for them and spent a total of five million yen on their training, and later one of them took in 90 million yen at one stroke in an unlisted shares scam. Guys like me were given that training too. But when I look at these kids nowadays, I feel sad that they're just disposable goods." Saying this, Chikushi's shoulders drooped.

5.10 The era of scam's internal collapse

Is this the bell tolling the death of the fraud enterprise? An era of internal collapse has appeared in the fraud business, of which preying on the elderly is representative. They did not succumb when the police devoted their full strength to investigating and unmasking the leaders, but are they foundering after all because of their internal distortions? That is not the case at all.

Kanbe, the former backer who appeared in the previous chapter, made this parting shot: "This is just a period of transition."

"In the end, everybody who has had experience as a *bantō* or higher up had been predicting that this business would be shaken up by the yakuza, haven't they? But even if the yakuza get involved, if you just accept that, in the end it just means that the number of guys feeding at this trough has increased, but nothing has changed. Rather, it would be unnatural for the scam organizations to assume a mutual hands-off policy; in the end, what seems to be happening is just that if the yakuza consolidate the strong and weak organizations, we'll be left with just a few really high-level organizations that will attract both the money and the talent, linking up a variety of gangs.

"Even if the number of organizations and the number

of cells decreases, it's just because outlaws are involved that there is a violent weeding out process that is not allowed in the normal world, so without any argument only the strongest remain."

This prediction is to be expected from Kanbe, who survived a tough situation, and it is rather preceptive. In the usual society, it takes many years for organizations to weed themselves out and for an industry to reorganize, but in the underground business world, that proceeds at an amazing pace to the end result.

At the end of the transition period and the weeding out, probably the business of preying on the elderly will become even more sophisticated and bare its fangs toward society. The players in the cells of the organizations that have survived the weeding out have been chosen by an even more severe selection process and engage in the fraud business with an even stronger sense of themselves as professionals, and a sense of being among the chosen. In the generation of player candidates, the more the trend towards becoming mild *yankī* who put up with low incomes spreads, the more the young people who do not accept that and have outstanding aspirations to better themselves will be attracted to this business more selectively.

This is Kanbe's assessment.

5.11 Wasted human resources and talent

What do you think? This is the present and future mentality of the young people who work in the organizations and cells of special fraud crimes, the apex of preying on the elderly. "What a waste of human resources and talent." This was my final thought after interviewing them.

In any case, the young people who are assigned as players to the scam cells are human resources that could achieve results in a variety of fields if they were given an environment in which they could act easily and provided with suitable training. However, the scam cells allow them to mature efficiently but on the other hand consume them with an extraordinary force. Kanbe, quoted above, has seen many rank-and-file players and what happened to them afterward, had this to say: "More than half the players break down."

"I myself went through a period of uncertainty. First, many scam cells are the short-term decisive battle type. You work intensively for two months and then you rest for several months until you get the next call. During that time, a lot of guys go stale.

"However severely they are warned by the *bantō* and the cell managers, some turn to dope, or cut loose so much that they're noticed by some yakuza and are beaten up, or they hang out at casinos and lose several million yen in one night at baccarat. One of the conditions for my promotion to *bantō* was that I had been saving my money, but for most of the players, they'd be lucky if they still had half of what they'd earned. These jerks get lazy during the waiting period, so when they're suddenly assigned to a new cell it takes some time before they can come up to speed. There're a lot of guys who earned the most at their first cell, and then gradually their earnings drop. For players, it's not just simply the number of years of experience."

On the other hand, however mature they may appear, most players are youths in their 20s. It is said that the more genuine they are, the harder they fall after they give up being a player and become an average citizen.

"In the end, there's no kind of work that rewards effort more than the scam business. To begin with, the unit labor cost is different. First, a guy who is employed at a typical job can't do it for a while. It makes me laugh. On top of that, and this applies to me too, if you compare the guys in a scam cell with people in other companies, I get so I want to thrash them, their motivation is so low. Therefore, most former players don't choose to get a job somewhere, but this too ends in a big failure. For example, they invest money to open a restaurant or bar, or there are guys who are consultants for opening crooked businesses clearly targeting former scam players, or they open a cabaret or a sex business, but these don't last a year, and so they piss away several million or several tens of million yen of their capital. That's the standard pattern."

Many players, after leaving the business, grumble that they would like to become players again, but they don't really try to do it until the money they previously earned has been exhausted. For this reason, among the former players that Kanbe has seen, are those who are spending a really horrible time as alcoholics, drug addicts, compulsive gamblers, or online game addicts.

I felt the truth of what he said because among the former scammers I met in the course of my research were some who had come to rack and ruin. When you consider that formerly they too had been displaying their talents to the maximum with the bizarre motivation characterizing the scam cells, you have to conclude that, after all, this is a waste. There are some who, returning to a cell several years after they had retired, cannot keep up with the rapidly changing situation in the cells, and are treated there as excess baggage or interfering old-timers. It is just like seeing the decline of a star player in the sports world after retirement.

Further, I have also heard that recently, such former players and those who have left the cells and are working as recruiters, sending their juniors to the scam cells as players, are being approached by the yakuza proactively and are being urged to register as gang members. For the yakuza, who are struggling with a shortage of young candidates for membership, former scammers are evaluated as outstanding talent who can lead the underworld in the future.

Formerly, this "chivalrous group" had an aspect of bringing those who could not survive in the world into the family and feeding them, and in return making them pledge themselves to the family (i.e., the gang), but now the ironic situation was appearing of the underworld salvaging the outstanding talent that had been left behind by society at large. However, it goes without saying that the recent severe clamping down on the chivalrous groups' (antisocial forces') economic activities is a factor here. Talented young people who have escaped the stifling environment of the fraud business are thrust again into a different oppressive environment.

I cannot help feeling that it is really too cruel to say that they brought it on themselves.

5.12 Young people who are abandoned and cornered

Young people, who are this country's treasure, are taken into these criminal organizations and consumed there, and then fresh young talent is taken in; the organizations are restructured, and so the business of preying on the elderly will never end.

For more than ten years since special fraud crimes became rampant in Japan, I have continued to interview young people working in a variety of scam cells. At first, I thought that this was simply just an unground part-time job, and some really unruly brats were emerging. However, gradually, I began to think that they arose of necessity in present-day Japan.

The total amount of losses from preying on the elderly (i.e., special fraud crimes) will reach 50 billion yen in the first eleven months of 2014. However, I believe that the loss to society in the long term caused by the situation that forces these young men into the business of preying on the elderly is greater than this amount.

Of course, not all of the elderly are well-off; there are disparities within the elderly generation. Many elderly persons suffer from poverty. There are some who suffer as victims. However, it is none other than the young players preying on the elderly who are Japan's precious working population whose remaining years of active service is the next 30 or 40 years.

"One must not steal" "One must not cheat"; the younger generation has been forced into going so far as to break these natural restraints, and the result is the prevalence of preying on the elderly. Isn't it too irresponsible just to moan that the world has become a really terrible place as if it were someone else's problem? Because in such a world it is none other than the elderly themselves, who have now become the target of these crimes, who have created the Japan that ignores and shuts out these young people.

Afterword

I have seen young people who work in remittance fraud cells reading business magazines that target seniors. They read such magazines to learn the psychology of their victims, and the trends affecting the elderly today. One article, printed in such large type it can be read even by the farsighted, was a special feature on how to select a high-priced private retirement home.

"If there's an elderly person who can afford a 50-million-yen entry fee, I could probably take five million in one shot with a scam about an initial installment of the entry fee. Just thinking about it makes me really happy!"

This young man was a compassionate person who valued above all his friends and his girlfriend, but he had come to think that the group of people who could be called the rich elderly were not even humans who lived on the same planet that he did.

The greying society is a society in which a small number of young people are supporting a large number of old people who have lost their productive power. Further, the economic gap between the young and the elderly, which has widened to an unprecedented degree, and the worldview of today's young people, whose efforts are hardly rewarded, necessarily have given rise to young people who choose to take rather than support. This is preying on the elderly.

That sentiment is no different from that shown by young people who display a negative feeling towards paying towards a pension that they may never receive in the future. If it were not for the proviso that it is a crime, any young person today could become a player for preying on the elderly. Their feelings of stagnation, hopelessness, discouragement, and resignation are deep. Of course, it is obvious that deceiving people and taking their money and goods (i.e., fraud) is a crime and as such cannot be encouraged. It certainly is an action that disturbs the social order, and their taking money from the elderly certainly does not make the world a better place. However, the one thing that can be said is that this would not have occurred if they had been given something before they took it.

Originally, what wealthy elderly people should have done is not only to pay for their children's and grandchildren's education and toil, but also to spend money and make efforts to bring up the entire generation of young people who will be supporting their own generation in the future, and to provide them with a supportive environment, energy, and hopes. However, the actuality is completely the opposite. Until now, rather than raising all the issues and making policies for developing productivity in the future with social systems to support the young generation, solve the tuition problem, and support parents with young children, the priority destination for spending money always has been the problems of the elderly. Respect for the aged and despising the young has become established to a shocking degree.

The method that will lead to a resolution of preying on the elderly in the future will not be by anti-crime measures nor by enlightening people about their techniques. I believe that it can be done only by providing for and bringing up future generations.

www.ingramcontent.com/pod-product-compliance
Lightning Source LLC
Chambersburg PA
CBHW071720140626
46557CB00012B/976